WEB 3.0

www.royalcollins.com

WEB 3.0

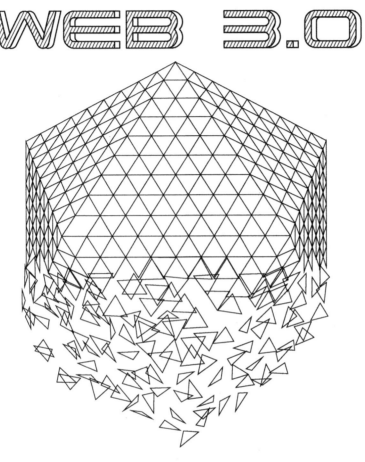

THE FUTURE OF DECENTRALIZED INTERNET

Kevin Chen

Books Beyond Boundaries

ROYAL COLLINS

Web 3.0: The Future of Decentralized Internet

Kevin Chen

First published in 2024 by Royal Collins Publishing Group Inc.
Groupe Publication Royal Collins Inc.
550-555 boul. René-Lévesque O Montréal (Québec) H2Z1B1 Canada

10 9 8 7 6 5 4 3 2 1

ISBN: 978-1-4878-1181-5

To find out more about our publications, please visit www.royalcollins.com.

Contents

Contents

Contents

Prologue

November 23 marks the fourteenth day since Amy's discharge from the hospital. Two weeks ago, while racing with her classmates in the evening, she failed to notice an iron fence on the path. In her haste, she collided with it—her one thigh made it over while the other didn't, resulting in her flipping over and landing harshly on the ground. She regained consciousness in a hospital bed.

It was from her classmates that Amy pieced together the events of that night. Her thigh had landed awkwardly, and the impact caused her nose to bleed profusely. It was a distressing realization. Thankfully, the subsequent surgery and rehabilitation went smoothly. Amy was back on her feet two days after the surgery, starting her rehabilitation exercises. She was discharged on the third-day post-operation.

On day fourteen post-discharge, Amy engages in daily rehabilitation and recovery exercises. These are essential for the quick healing of her thigh and her swift return to everyday life.

At 7:00 a.m., a home robot wakes Amy up. She stretches, sits up, and prepares for her rehabilitation routine. A small display screen beside her bed connects to all her wearable smart devices, such as a smartwatch, smart ring, and smart vest, showing her health status and physiological data. Before the accident, Amy used to check her sleep quality and heart rate data every morning. Now, she also monitors her recovery progress and physical activity data.

"Good morning, Amy! Are you ready for today's rehabilitation training?" Kangyun, a rehab robot customized for Amy's recovery, moves toward her. It understands her injury and health status and can tailor rehabilitation exercises based on real-time data from her wearable devices.

Amy dons her sensor-equipped rehabilitation outfit, nodding to Kangyun, "Yes, I'm ready." In the days following her injury, Kangyun has become an indispensable companion, teaching her to manage pain, conduct proper exercises, and provide constant encouragement and support. Kangyun's presence has significantly expedited her recovery.

Kangyun then guides Amy through various stretching and strengthening exercises. Amy focuses on her breathing and each movement, executing the stretches slowly while her rehabilitation outfit records every motion's amplitude and frequency. This data is sent in real-time to Kangyun, which provides ongoing encouragement and advice, helping Amy adjust the intensity and angles of her movements for optimal rehabilitation effectiveness.

The one-and-a-half-hour rehabilitation session ends quickly. With each day's training, Amy feels her body steadily regaining its strength.

Besides her daily rehabilitation exercises, Amy has another critical task—recording her health data. Deciding to sell her health data for additional income to offset some medical expenses came naturally to her, having grown up in the Web 3.0 era.

Amy had read about the Web 2.0 era and found it hard to fathom not owning her digital identity and the data she generated. She appreciates the Web 3.0 era's commercial rules, where individual data isn't just stored passively on large platforms' servers but is a valuable asset. Data transactions are transparent and equitable, allowing Amy to manage and utilize her data freely.

After each day's training, Amy compiles her treatment records, health metrics, and rehabilitation progress into a digital file, which she then uploads to a personal data trading platform. This platform enables her to sell her health data to medical institutions, insurance companies, and research organizations. For medical institutions, this data aids in understanding patients' conditions and treatment processes, allowing for more personalized medical services. For insurance companies, it helps assess Amy's health and risk levels to formulate appropriate policies. Research organizations might use the data to support medical studies.

Though her injury was unfortunate, trading her health data has brought Amy a substantial income, turning an adverse situation into a beneficial experience.

However, this scenario is not our current reality. While Amy lives in the Web 3.0 era in this narrative, we still inhabit a Web 2.0 world, where personal data is monopolized by centralized entities, and data ownership and trading are in their infancy. Yet, there's a substantial anticipation for the Web 3.0 era, which is seen as inevitable and irreversible, both from technological trends and the evolution of human civilization. Achieving Web 3.0 signifies digital sovereignty, where users are recognized as individuals, not merely as cogs in the data economy machine.

Now, let's embark on this journey through the book to explore the imminent Web 3.0 era and the approaching age of digital sovereignty.

PART ONE

The Web 3.0 Vision in the Web 2.0 Era

What exactly is Web 3.0? At its core, it signifies the forthcoming wave of Internet evolution. Yet, the full scope of this evolution is a bit like trying to grasp the vastness of the metaverse—our current technological standpoint doesn't quite capture the impending societal transformation, particularly as ongoing tech advancements continually reshape our vision of this still-forming future.

Tracing the digital arc from Web 1.0 through Web 2.0, the surge of mobile Internet, and now toward the cusp of Web 3.0, we're witnessing a series of inevitable tech breakthroughs. However, our grasp of what Web 3.0 will truly embody if constrained by today's tech frameworks remains fundamentally limited and may not fully capture the essence of an authentic Web 3.0 experience. The present discourse around Web 3.0 is predominantly blockchain-centric, with much of the conversation revolving around virtual currencies and decentralized digital models.

Yet, decentralization itself is just a concept. Absolute decentralization remains elusive as long as we operate within structured human societies. Concepts like centralization, much like freedom and democracy, are relative, reflecting specific historical and developmental contexts just as the Internet has nudged businesses toward some degree of decentralization—utilizing tech, particularly mobile Internet, to bypass traditional intermediaries, shifting toward a direct B to C model.

Peering into the Internet's evolution amid the surge of data and the monopolization of data and algorithms by platforms, it's evident we're stepping into the era of digital twins. We're transitioning from mere biological entities to beings with digital counterparts. The onset of this digital twin era heralds the need for digital identities and sovereignty, sparking an awakening of digital sovereignty consciousness. As data sovereignty becomes paramount, and individuals and communities realize its significance, a pushback against centralized data monopolies will take shape. This resistance will foster new business models rooted in technology and user data sovereignty—what we're defining as Web 3.0.

Can Web 3.0 truly herald an era of full decentralization or a centerless realm? The straightforward answer is no. Our aim should be a model where individual digital sovereignty is more pronounced, open, and freer than the prevalent platform-centric centralization. In essence, as long as governments and structured societal orders exist, operations will inherently adhere to some form of centralized rules. In the Web 3.0 epoch, decentralization is still a relative term, marking a shift from the current era where platforms dominate individual data rights—a shift driven by technological progress.

Many current discussions on Web 3.0, particularly those anchored in blockchain or Web 2.0 technologies, fail to fully embrace a next-gen Internet perspective. Blockchain, while a pivotal technology in transitioning from Web 2.0 to 3.0, doesn't epitomize decentralization but is a sophisticated response to the burgeoning data landscape. Yet, these complex encryption technologies might soon become antiquated when juxtaposed with quantum computing.

Thus, delving into Web 3.0 demands a forward-thinking tech perspective, considering advancements like quantum computing, quantum communication, space-based communication, DNA storage, digital twins, and metaverse technologies. This book unfolds in two segments: the initial part tackles Web 3.0 from today's tech lens, especially through blockchain, portraying it as the Web 3.0 vision within a Web 2.0 framework.

The subsequent, more pivotal segment, examines Web 3.0 through the prism of leading-edge or foreseeable tech trends, defining it as the Web 3.0 vision for the Web 3.0 era itself. Like my metaverse discussions, present portrayals feel more like speculative narratives since the foundational tech for constructing the metaverse remains in development. The metaverse, propelled by digital twin tech, signifies a new interconnected form, an evolution from the melding of physical and digital twin worlds. Describing this future from our current tech standpoint is challenging; a more accurate forecast hinges on an understanding rooted in emerging tech trends.

In essence, for Web 3.0, a lucid and precise vision requires a foundation in imminent cutting-edge tech trends. Yet, it's clear that any projections of Web 3.0 based solely on today's Web 2.0 tech will appear dated and old-fashioned when the genuine Web 3.0 era unfolds.

—CHAPTER 1—

An Introduction to Web 3.0

1.1 The Past, Present, and Future of the Internet

The Internet is a monumental technological achievement of our era, profoundly influencing every facet of our personal, professional, and societal lives. An American writer, Henry Hardy once hailed the Internet as "a unique creation of human intelligence, the first product of human intellect. It signals a new society growing within the old, proposes new modes of governance, poses threats to the freedoms of civil society, and is the largest free market of ideas and thoughts . . . The Internet is immortal." Indeed, the Internet has experienced significant transformations since its inception, evolving from the portal-focused Web 1.0 to the interactive Web 2.0. Now, we're on the brink of embracing a decentralized Web 3.0 amid ongoing innovations in various information technologies.

1.1.1 Web 1.0: The Internet of the Portal Era

Web 1.0, the inaugural phase of the Internet, was publicized in the 1990s. Still, its roots extend back to 1968 with the inception of ARPANET (Advanced Research Projects Agency Network), a US government initiative. ARPANET was originally a modest network where military contractors and university scholars exchanged data.

During the late 1950s, amid the Cold War tensions, the US military aimed to ensure uninterrupted network communication even during an attack, giving rise to the military network known as ARPANET. Activated in 1969, it initially linked four computers to facilitate networking experiments among scientists. By the 1970s, ARPANET expanded into multiple computer networks, yet they lacked interconnectivity. To overcome this, ARPA embarked on new research projects to interlink distinct local computer networks, culminating in creating the "Internet."

Communication protocols, particularly the Transmission Control Protocol / Internet Protocol (TCP/IP) introduced in 1974, were pivotal in achieving network interconnectivity. Vinton Cerf and Bob Kahn, key figures in designing the TCP/IP protocol and Internet architecture, are often celebrated as the "fathers of the Internet." The principle of openness in TCP/IP was designed to enable communication across computers from various manufacturers, rendering the Internet an open system. The burgeoning interest from the commercial sector in the Internet led to the establishment of the ANS network by IBM, MCI, and MERIT in 1992, providing an additional backbone network.

The advent of the World Wide Web significantly lowered the barriers to Internet usage by integrating client/server model-based information discovery and hypertext technologies, which allowed for interlinking sites. Tim Berners-Lee, the web inventor, played a pivotal role in the information revolution, drastically altering access to information worldwide, and is thus esteemed as another "father of the Internet."

His invention revolutionized global information dissemination, propelling the information revolution and turning the Internet into a vast ocean of globally accessible knowledge, encompassing all facets of social production and life. Initially an internal communication technology for the US military, the Internet was commercialized and released to the public during President Clinton's tenure to rejuvenate the American economy, heralding the Internet era for humanity. This marked the beginning of the Internet age in the 1990s, with Web 1.0 serving as the first developmental stage of the Internet, continuing into the early 21st century.

During the Web 1.0 phase, users were mere content consumers, with content provided by websites. This era's websites resembled digitized newspapers or TV channels, transferring news and advertisements online and offering information unilaterally to users. User interaction was limited to choosing websites, searching for desired content, and receiving and processing data pushed by websites. This period saw the emergence of many familiar portals, search engines, and forums, like Yahoo, Sohu, NetEase, and Google. Their common feature was providing content unilaterally to users, who primarily engaged in browsing and searching, with sites earning revenue through ad clicks.

In other words, during the Web 1.0 era, users passively received content from the Internet, experiencing minimal interaction. While not entirely devoid of interactive or payment functionalities, these were significantly restricted due to insecure transaction infrastructures. The late Web 1.0 era did witness the advent of instant messaging, predominantly through web-based chat rooms utilized in various forums, like Tsinghua University's SMTH BBS and Xiaonei in mainland China. One of the most innovative companies of this era was Pizza Hut in the United States, which developed a webpage in 1995 for pizza ordering, allowing customers to place orders online and pay upon delivery.

Web 1.0 primarily functioned as an information dissemination platform, where users used website browsers to access and retrieve information. In mobile devices, this era was marked by activities such as reading novels on 2G networks or listening to music over 3G connections; applications were predominantly designed for reading, with content creation playing a secondary role.

From a business standpoint, the profit model during Web 1.0 hinged on user attention and clicks—users engaged with information on web pages, and service providers generated revenue through advertising and page views. Users spent time acquiring information, yet the opportunities for individual profit-making were limited.

As the Internet user base burgeoned, the constraints of Web 1.0 became increasingly conspicuous. The era was marked by limited customization and personalization; the static nature of web pages curtailed users' ability to adapt content to their preferences and needs. Interactivity was minimal, with websites focusing more on presenting information rather than enabling user interaction. The absence of direct engagement features like comments, shares, and likes led to reduced user engagement and a diminished social experience online. Moreover, with the growing prevalence of the Internet, users face the challenge of information overload. The deluge of data, coupled with Web 1.0's lack of effective filtering and recommendation systems, made it arduous for users to discover relevant or interesting content. Additionally, the business model's monotony—relying solely on advertisements and clicks—prompted websites to prioritize boosting page views, often at the expense of providing valuable or authentic content. This approach targeted user attention, frequently leaving users with scant substantive value in return.

In response to these limitations, the stage was set for the advent of Web 2.0.

1.1.2 Web 2.0: The Interactive Internet

Web 2.0, or the second generation of the Internet, was introduced in late 2004 by Tim O'Reilly and Dale Dougherty. The advent of Web 2.0 aimed to address the limitations of Web 1.0, with its most significant advancement being the transition of users from passive content viewers to active content creators and sharers.

A defining feature of Web 2.0 is user engagement and feedback—users can upload their content and interact with others' content through comments, likes, and shares. This bidirectional interactivity transformed the Internet from a mere channel for information delivery into a vibrant and dynamic social platform. Users were no longer just spectators; they actively participated in content creation and distribution.

Interactive websites became the hallmark of the Web 2.0 era, moving away from static pages to ones filled with user participation. Social networking sites, blogs, and wikis exemplified Web 2.0 applications, offering platforms for information sharing and igniting user creativity and engagement.

This starkly contrasted to Web 1.0, where websites primarily facilitated connection and sharing. Web 2.0 evolved from this foundation, enabling closer connections among users through social media interactions and forming various online communities. The Internet evolved from a unidirectional flow of information to a multidimensional and multilayered exchange network.

Web 2.0's emergence was undoubtedly fueled by advancements in Internet technologies, such as improved Internet speeds, fiber-optic infrastructure, and search engines, which attracted more users to the Internet, increasing demand for social networking, music, video sharing, and online transactions.

This demand led to the rise of many Internet enterprises. Platforms like Facebook (now Meta), Twitter (now X), WeChat, and Weibo provided social networking functionalities, while Napster, YouTube, and TikTok catered to music and video sharing needs.

Taking Sina Weibo as an example, it represents a typical Web 2.0 social media platform based on user relationships. Users could access Weibo via various mobile devices to share, disseminate, and interact with information in real-time using text, images, videos, and other multimedia formats.

Four key characteristics of Weibo highlight the essence of Web 2.0: low entry barriers, enabling anyone to publish content, thus democratizing media creation; rapid dissemination, with information spreading swiftly among users; personalization, where users receive tailored content based on their interests and interactions; and interactivity, fostering a more engaging Internet experience.

However, Web 2.0's interactive experience, despite enhancing functionalities and user experience, introduced issues that persist today. Users had to entrust their data to centralized third-party platforms to access these new features, granting these entities significant power over data and content. This centralization concentrated communication and commercial activities within a few tech giants' platforms, such as Google, Meta, and Amazon, a trend that continues today. What's more, in the centralized realm of Web 2.0, individuals find their lives deeply intertwined with digital platforms, leading to a dilution of the Internet's original promise of democratization. The integrity of information has waned, occasionally veering into detrimental territories. Users face the reality of their data being traded or exploited without informed consent, introducing substantial concerns around privacy, data concentration, and management. The unchecked proliferation of misinformation, coupled with the societal quandaries posed by artificial intelligence (AI)-crafted deepfakes and identity theft, underscores the urgency for the next Internet evolution—Web 3.0.

The evolutionary leap from Web 1.0 and Web 2.0 to the forthcoming Web 3.0 is fundamentally propelled by technological progress. The development of Internet software and hardware is birthing novel business models. In this light, the amalgamation of disruptive technologies like quantum computing, quantum communication, DNA storage, space-based communication, digital twinning, and artificial general intelligence (AGI) heralds a transformative era for industries anchored in Web technologies.

Web 3.0 is not a distant possibility but an impending reality deserving of anticipation rather than skepticism. While our present grasp of Web 3.0 might not fully encapsulate its eventual manifestation, it's clear that the complexity of Web 3.0, with its reliance on an array of advanced technologies, marks a significant departure from its predecessors. Each of these technologies, reaching maturity, holds the potential to revolutionize society in a manner akin to a seismic shift.

In the subsequent section, I'll explore the essence and prospective landscape of Web 3.0 in greater depth, offering insights into what this new Internet chapter could entail.

1.1.3 Web 3.0: The Decentralized Internet

Not long after Ethereum's debut in 2014, its co-founder Gavin Wood introduced the term "Web 3.0" in a blog post, exploring the revolutionary potential of a decentralized Internet. This concept, like Web 2.0 before it, arose from a need to resolve pressing concerns of the current Internet, particularly issues of privacy and trust infringed upon by governments and technology giants. Wood advocated for a more reliable, decentralized Internet, envisioning Web 3.0 as the pathway to achieving this. Anchored in blockchain technology, Web 3.0 aims to restore privacy and digital identity to individuals, fostering novel interactions through non-fungible tokens (NFTs) and decentralized applications (dApps).

Blockchain, known for its robust security and decentralized nature, enables the storage of data, exchange of value, and recording of transactions on a shared ledger beyond the control of any single entity. Serving as the infrastructure of Web 3.0, blockchain provides a secure platform for creating, issuing, and trading cryptographic assets and crafting programmable smart contracts.

These smart contracts, immutable code on the blockchain, autonomously execute transactions based on predefined conditions, facilitating the development of dApps. These dApps, foundational to Web 3.0, empower users by offering a new level of control.

Distinct from the centralized applications of Web 2.0 or the static pages of Web 1.0, dApps operate on a decentralized blockchain network, enabling the establishment of complex automated systems, including peer-to-peer financial services, data-centric insurance offerings, and Play-to-Earn (P2E) games.

With their unique, indivisible nature, NFTs differ from fungible cryptocurrencies like Bitcoin. Blockchain technology ensures that the originality and exclusivity of an NFT can be authenticated, despite possible copies or screenshots, through digital certificates of ownership.

Web 3.0, championing decentralization and enhanced interactivity, cultivates a new Internet paradigm where users interact directly, eliminating the need for intermediaries. dApp users can freely access financial tools, engage in peer-to-peer cryptocurrency exchanges, secure insurance payouts, trade-in digitally authenticated art via NFTs, and monetize gaming activities—all without central oversight. The aim is to build a more equitable, transparent Internet where direct user interactions and transactions are the norm.

In essence, Web 3.0 disrupts the centralized dominance of tech giants characterizing the Web 2.0 era. In this new landscape, blockchain-based platforms and applications are not controlled by corporations but by their user communities, who contribute to their growth and sustainment, thereby earning a stake in them.

Web 3.0 is heralded as the forthcoming Internet evolution, encapsulating a vision of decentralization and user empowerment. It represents an Internet with information access independent of intermediaries like ISPs, Google, or Facebook. In the Web 3.0 world, individuals can communicate directly, maintaining ownership of their data instead of trading it for "free" services. With Web 3.0, the Internet is set to become smarter and more decentralized, transforming how we interact with the digital world.

1.2 Core Features of Web 3.0

Currently, Web 3.0 embodies a transformative shift, heralding a reimagined and enhanced vision for the Internet. Its essence lies in leveraging blockchain technology, cryptocurrencies, and dApps to empower and grant ownership back to users. In simple terms, Web 1.0 allowed users to read, Web 2.0 added the ability to write, and the forward-looking Web 3.0 introduced the ability to own.

While a universally accepted definition of Web 3.0 is yet to be established, with varying interpretations among different organizations and individuals, contrasting Web 2.0 and Web 3.0 elucidates how this forthcoming iteration of the Internet diverges from our present Web 2.0 experience. This comparison offers insights into the defining characteristics of Web 3.0 and the anticipated future.

1.2.1 Technological Logical Differences

Each Internet generation has its own set of protocols, the basic rules and agreements for Internet communication, defining how data is exchanged and transmitted between computers.

In today's Web 2.0, the most familiar protocol is HTTP (Hypertext Transfer Protocol), a client-server protocol facilitating user interactions with web servers. This model, where the client (typically a web browser) sends requests to servers, which respond, has become foundational to Internet use, allowing easy access to various websites and web applications.

HTTP's popularity stems from its widespread use and compatibility with all web browsers, enabling developers to easily create web applications that function across different devices and browsers. This universality has contributed to the Internet's openness and accessibility, as users don't need to worry about using specific browsers to access certain websites.

However, HTTP has limitations like all technologies, such as scalability challenges. Under massive data transfer and storage demands, HTTP may exhibit inefficiencies. Traditional HTTP can face latency and performance bottlenecks when handling large-scale data, potentially hampering efficiency in today's Internet, where large media files and dynamic content are commonplace.

Security limitations are another consideration for HTTP. The protocol transmits data in plaintext, making it susceptible to network attacks. While HTTP Secure emerged to enhance security by encrypting communication, potential risks still linger even with encrypted protection.

Amid these challenges, emerging technologies and protocols, like IPFS (InterPlanetary File System) from Web 3.0, are gaining attention as potential solutions to HTTP's issues.

IPFS is a distributed protocol that transforms a file storage system into a vast library rather than a single file cabinet. Traditional networks store files on specific servers, requiring knowledge of their exact location. In contrast, IPFS, like a library, locates files by content, not location. Files are broken into pieces, each with a unique identifier, enabling content retrieval via the IPFS protocol regardless of specific locations, embodying decentralization. Files aren't concentrated in one place but can exist simultaneously in multiple locations, enhancing network flexibility.

This distributed architecture offers significant benefits, including enhanced security, as attacking multiple points is more challenging than targeting a centralized location. Efficiency is also improved, with faster access to files from nearer locations and reduced data loss or damage risks due to multiple backups. For instance, in a traditional network, finding a specific book requires knowing its exact cabinet location. With IPFS, you need only the book's unique identifier, allowing quicker access to the information you seek. By altering file storage and retrieval methods, IPFS achieves decentralization, bolstering network security and efficiency.

Another protocol in Web 3.0 is the Whisper protocol in the Ethereum network, facilitating peer-to-peer message exchanges among nodes. Whisper offers a decentralized alternative to traditional messaging services aimed at security, efficiency, and scalability.

Beyond these, Web 3.0 has developed various decentralized data-sharing platforms and applications, like Ocean Protocol and Golem, enabling secure and efficient data and computational resource sharing. These protocols highlight that while protocols inherently centralize rules, the push toward decentralization in Web 3.0 fosters a more open, freer information exchange system than the current platform-centric model.

1.2.2 Differences in Data Sharing and Storage

As the Internet has matured, various protocols have emerged, setting standards for how information is transmitted and exchanged and defining unique data sharing and storage methods.

Web 2.0 has been dominated by the traditional client-server model in data sharing. Here, a central server is the primary repository, managing and storing all the data. Client devices connect to this server to request and retrieve data, with the server orchestrating the data transactions. While this centralized approach has its conveniences, it also faces scalability issues, as all data must pass through a single point, potentially causing congestion and bottlenecks in performance. Moreover, centralizing data storage introduces significant security vulnerabilities, making the data a prime target for cyberattacks and raising the stakes for potential data breaches and manipulations.

Web 3.0, however, pioneers a shift in data sharing paradigms—embracing decentralized data sharing. Unlike the centralized model, this approach eschews a single server to distribute data across a peer-to-peer network. This decentralization offers marked improvements in security, transparency, and efficiency in data sharing. Utilizing blockchain technology, decentralized data sharing guarantees the immutability and integrity of data, with each block in the chain uniquely identified and secured, making the data resilient to tampering. Furthermore, removing intermediaries minimizes the risks associated with data breaches and manipulations, enhancing the overall security of the data ecosystem.

Web 3.0's decentralized data sharing also fosters data ownership and control, enabling individuals to share and monetize their data on their terms. Web 3.0 data sharing protocols are designed to be distributed across multiple nodes, achieving greater resilience, scalability, and security. This dispersed network structure is realized using blockchain technology and other peer-to-peer protocols, allowing secure and transparent data sharing without central authorities.

Regarding data storage, Web 2.0 and Web 3.0 exhibit clear distinctions. In Web 2.0, data is typically stored on centralized servers controlled by large corporations, utilizing SQL databases, NoSQL databases, and file systems.

SQL databases, relational in nature, store data in tables with columns and rows. They are widely used in Web 2.0 applications for structured data, including user profiles, transaction records, and inventory data. NoSQL databases, non-relational, store data in flexible formats like key-value pairs, documents, or graphs, catering to unstructured data like social media posts, product reviews, and sensor data. File systems manage unstructured data like images, videos, and documents, relying on centralized servers or Storage Area Networks in Web 2.0.

While Web 2.0 storage technologies have been successful in facilitating data storage and retrieval, they face limitations in security, privacy, and accessibility. Centralized storage systems are vulnerable to data breaches, surveillance, and system downtimes, requiring significant trust in the central entities managing the data.

In Web 3.0, however, data is decentralized and distributed across a network of nodes, primarily utilizing cryptographic protocols, peer-to-peer networks, and blockchain technology for data storage and management, enhancing security, privacy, and accessibility.

IPFS, for example, is a decentralized file storage system allowing users to store and share files across a network of nodes. It employs content addressing instead of location-based addressing, enabling more efficient and secure file storage and retrieval.

Swarm, a decentralized storage platform part of the Ethereum ecosystem, enables data storage and retrieval across a peer-to-peer network of nodes, with the added benefit of using smart contracts for data management and access. Using blockchain technology, Filecoin, another decentralized storage network, incentivizes users to contribute storage space and bandwidth. Users earn tokens by providing storage space and can use these tokens to access storage services others offer.

1.2.3 Advancements in Internet Security

The different technological logic and network structures between Web 2.0 and Web 3.0 result in significant differences in security. Web 2.0, a centralized system, is susceptible to various security risks, while Web 3.0 employs advanced security strategies through a decentralized architecture and encryption technologies, enhancing network security and resilience.

Centralized systems predominated in the Web 2.0 era, with data typically stored on central servers. However, this centralization made the system more vulnerable to various security issues.

Data breaches are a common risk in the Web 2.0 stage, affecting virtually everyone today. Personal information can mysteriously fall into the hands of organizations, often because all data is concentrated on a central server. Once compromised, an attacker can access a wealth of sensitive information, including personal details, payment data, and corporate secrets, posing direct threats to privacy and potentially leading to significant financial and reputational damages.

Identity theft is another serious concern. With personal information stored in central databases, breaches can provide attackers with sufficient details to impersonate identities, leading to financial losses, credit card fraud, and severe impacts on individuals' personal and financial well-being.

Additionally, distributed denial-of-service (DDoS) attacks are common in the Web 2.0 era. Attackers can overload servers by sending many simultaneous requests, disrupting service availability. Due to the centralized nature of these systems, a single point of failure can cause system-wide collapse, making Web 2.0 infrastructures attractive targets for attacks.

In the Web 2.0 era, security protocols relied heavily on SSL/TLS to protect data transmission over the Internet. While SSL/TLS provides encryption to secure data in transit, ensuring it isn't intercepted or altered, this alone is insufficient for complete security.

SSL/TLS focuses on encrypting end-to-end communications but does not fully protect data during storage and processing, where it may be decrypted and vulnerable. Furthermore, while SSL/TLS employs certificates to verify identities, it's still susceptible to man-in-the-middle attacks, where attackers intercept and alter communications.

Moreover, SSL/TLS's reliance on centralized certificate authorities presents a singular target for attacks, potentially compromising the entire system's security. While SSL/TLS ensures data confidentiality, it doesn't sufficiently safeguard data integrity, leaving room for potential alterations even during encrypted transmissions.

Contrastingly, Web 3.0's decentralized architecture and encryption enhance security significantly. Decentralization is foundational to Web 3.0's security, distributing data across multiple nodes. Each node participates in data storage and transmission, creating a robust dispersed network against attacks. Attackers must compromise multiple nodes simultaneously, a far more challenging feat than targeting a single centralized server.

Web 3.0 also extensively employs cryptographic technologies to ensure data encryption during transmission and storage. Even if data is intercepted, decryption is difficult without the corresponding keys. Strong encryption algorithms in Web 3.0 mitigate risks of data breaches and identity theft.

Furthermore, Web 3.0's use of blockchain technology enhances data immutability and transparency. Blockchain's distributed, tamper-proof ledger ensures data integrity; altering data is nearly impossible once recorded. Transparency means all participants can view and verify data, increasing system trustworthiness.

Web 3.0 also employs cryptographic methods, such as public-private key encryption and digital signatures, to authenticate identities and maintain data integrity. Users have private keys for decryption and public keys for encryption and signing, preventing identity theft and data tampering. Public-private key encryption ensures only the keyholder can decrypt data, while digital signatures verify data remains unaltered during transmission.

1.2.4 Differences in Web Applications

Web 2.0 and Web 3.0 application architectures are markedly different, influenced by their respective protocols, network constructions, and security measures.

In the traditional web application architecture, the client-server model is prevalent, where clients send requests to servers, who process and respond to these requests. This model centralizes data and business logic on the server side, with clients mainly handling the user interface presentation. Such centralization relies heavily on centralized control and trust.

However, the Web 3.0 era introduces a novel architecture: dApps. Built upon blockchain technology, these dApps execute smart contracts automatically, facilitating trustless, transparent, and secure applications. Smart contracts, which automatically execute contractual rules and stipulations, play a crucial role in dApps.

On the one hand, smart contracts enable dApps to establish decentralized autonomous systems, breaking free from central control reliance. In traditional architectures, the server acts as the steward of data and business rules. When using an app, your device (client) communicates with this steward to request data retrieval or action execution. The steward processes these requests and returns the results.

In dApps, however, this logic is embedded in smart contracts, replacing the steward's role. Smart contracts are specialized computational codes residing on the blockchain, a public ledger recording all transactions and operations. When you initiate a request in a dApp, it bypasses the need for a central server. Instead, smart contracts, like automatic rulebooks containing the app's business logic and operational rules, process your request. It's sent to the blockchain, where the smart contract executes the relevant rules, generates results, and logs them on the blockchain. This concept of "establishing decentralized autonomous systems" means that the app's logic isn't centralized on one server but is distributed among various blockchain nodes via smart contracts. This decentralization reduces reliance on a single control point, automating various app operations with smart contracts.

Furthermore, smart contracts facilitate new business models. Smart contracts can create diverse commercial logic, including intermediary-free transactions and trustless collaborations, fostering innovation and more open, efficient trade mechanisms by leveraging blockchain's transparency and programmability.

For instance, consider traditional market shopping, where an intermediary, like a salesperson, is involved. In the smart contract world, the contract acts as an automated set of market rules, handling commercial logic directly. Your purchasing needs are coded into the smart contract, which executes market rules automatically, with blockchain's transparency allowing anyone to verify these rules, ensuring fairness and clarity. The programmability of smart contracts enables flexible adjustment to market rules based on varying needs and situations.

This approach, "promoting new business models," offers a decentralized, trustless mechanism for commercial transactions, removing the cumbersome processes of traditional intermediaries and enabling more direct, efficient trade. Imagine future rental transactions without intermediaries, where smart contracts contain rental rules, facilitating automatic payment and access provision upon meeting set conditions. This method streamlines the rental process, bypassing cumbersome interactions and trust issues between tenants and landlords.

Additionally, the smart contracts within the dApp ecosystem are characterized by openness and accountability. Since they operate on the blockchain, all contract executions are publicly verifiable, enhancing system transparency. This means participants can oversee contract execution, establishing a fairer and more accountable system.

1.2.5 Differences in Digital Identity

The digital identity landscape is markedly different between the Web 2.0 and Web 3.0 eras. Currently, we juggle multiple accounts across various platforms like Twitter, YouTube, Douyin, and Kuaishou, each necessitating a distinct registration process. When users wish to update their personal details, such as a nickname, avatar, or background image, they're required to individually log into each platform to make these changes. Though some platforms offer consolidated logins via a single email or social media account, this raises concerns regarding privacy and surveillance.

The situation becomes more challenging if a social media giant decides to suspend a user's account on one platform, potentially impacting their presence on others. Furthermore, some platforms mandate the submission of real personal identification, like a national ID number, for account verification.

Web 3.0, however, streamlines this process significantly. In this new era, users can unify and manage their digital identities using Ethereum addresses and Ethereum Name Service profiles. This means that one Ethereum address is sufficient for logging into multiple platforms, eliminating the need for separate accounts for each service. This Ethereum address acts as a unique identifier in the Web 3.0 realm, analogous to a real-life ID card. With this single digital address, users can navigate various online services without the repetitive hassle of multiple registrations and logins.

Moreover, this login method offers robust resistance to censorship, thanks to the blockchain infrastructure supporting Ethereum addresses. It's challenging for any single entity or institution to block or censor these addresses, granting users greater autonomy and resilience against external disruptions in online services. Additionally, this method enhances user privacy. Ethereum addresses do not directly associate with users' real-world identities, offering a layer of anonymity during cross-platform interactions, a notable shift from the Web 2.0 requirement of submitting genuine identity information for account registrations.

1.2.6 Differences in Payment Methods

In the Web 2.0 world, our payment systems are largely anchored in centralized institutions like banks and third-party payment processors, pivotal for facilitating transactions. Yet, as we transition into the Web 3.0 era, we're on the cusp of a significant overhaul in how payments are processed.

Web 3.0 introduces the utilization of cryptocurrencies, such as Ether, revolutionizing how transactions are conducted. This advancement allows individuals globally to execute payments directly within their browsers, provided they have an Internet connection, thanks to the decentralized essence of cryptocurrencies which mitigates the dependence on traditional banking systems or intermediary entities.

Here are the key shifts Web 3.0 brings to the payment landscape:

(1) Global accessibility. Cryptocurrencies like Ether ensure that anyone, anywhere with an Internet connection, can partake in transactions, dismantling geographical barriers and fostering enhanced freedom in international commerce.

(2) Enhanced security. Unlike the centralized validation process of Web 2.0, Web 3.0 leverages smart contracts and decen-

tralized frameworks to facilitate transparent, traceable, and secure transactions across the network. Smart contracts autonomously execute transactions upon the fulfillment of predefined conditions, bolstering trust and efficiency.

(3) Privacy preservation. Traditional payment systems often require the disclosure of substantial personal information. Web 3.0, however, allows for transactions to be made with cryptocurrencies without the necessity to reveal extensive personal details, augmenting the security and privacy of payments.

(4) Decentralized control. The Web 3.0 payment ecosystem isn't under the purview of any single entity. This starkly contrasts the Web 2.0 scenario where payment processors have the authority to scrutinize, censor, or freeze accounts. The decentralized nature of Web 3.0 payments diminishes reliance on intermediaries, granting users greater autonomy over their finances and mitigating the risks associated with monopolistic practices.

The distinctions between the present Web 2.0 and the forthcoming Web 3.0 are profound. Web 3.0 heralds a shift in technical logic, data sharing, storage methodologies, security protocols, application development, and digital identity management. Although still in nascent stages, Web 3.0 promises a radical transformation in our online interactions, aspiring to create a more open, transparent, and secure digital realm.

1.3 Rebuilding Trust—Web 3.0's Core Objective

The early visionaries of the Internet dreamt of a "digital utopia"—a realm where this burgeoning, accessible, and anonymous platform would nurture a decentralized, egalitarian, harmonious, and liberated society. The

Internet was heralded as a transformative technological marvel, capable of spawning unprecedented business models and ecosystems.

However, as we navigate through the Web 2.0 landscape, it becomes clear that this "digital utopia" has yet to come to fruition. The ideal of truly equal and open discourse remains a distant dream. A few tech giants now dominate the social media landscape, controlling over 90% of the market share. These entities monopolize conversations, set usage terms, and alter service conditions at their discretion, often leaving users with minimal influence or control. Furthermore, the digital world is plagued with data misuse and security breaches, eroding public trust.

Despite its indispensability, people's trust in the Internet has waned. It's within this backdrop that the concept of Web 3.0 has surfaced, championing the mission to restore faith in the digital domain. Web 3.0's narrative and ideology are profoundly ingrained, aspiring to resurrect the vision of the Internet that its pioneers envisaged—a realm where trust, transparency, and user empowerment are at the forefront.

1.3.1 The Founding Vision of the Internet

The dawn of the Internet was met with grand expectations and visions. On February 8, 1996, amid discussions surrounding the US Telecommunications Act of 1996, John Perry Barlow, co-founder of the Electronic Frontier Foundation, issued a seminal document titled "Declaration of the Independence of Cyberspace." This manifesto, which resonated deeply within early Internet circles, proclaimed, "Governments of the Industrial World, you weary giants of flesh and steel, I come from Cyberspace, the new home of Mind ... I declare the global social space we are building to be naturally independent of the tyrannies you seek to impose on us."

Barlow's declaration became a hallmark of tech determinism, encapsulating the utopian aspirations of the Internet's pioneers. They envisioned cyberspace as a distinct and autonomous realm, advocating for the diminishing influence of traditional power structures to allow burgeoning online communities to flourish. This perspective highlighted a certain defiance and revolutionary zeal prevalent among Internet users of the era, who saw it as a bastion for unrestrained expression and information exchange, free from the constraints of the conventional world and governmental oversight. Barlow's bold statement expressed skepticism toward established institutions, proposing that the Internet community could self-govern.

While there was a persistent hope that the Internet could function autonomously from "industrial governments," it's crucial to acknowledge that the technological infrastructure underpinning the Internet—including computers, smartphones, servers, and routers—remains inextricably linked to industrial production and is subject to regulatory frameworks. The journey of the Internet, from its inception to the present day, reflects a complex interplay between technology, society, and governance.

While the idea of an independent cyberspace didn't fully materialize, the optimism driven by tech determinism has significantly influenced Internet development.

In the Web 1.0 era, the Internet did foster rational and fair discourse. Users, who were relatively well-educated and financially stable given the era's limited access to technology, engaged in meaningful discussions in chat rooms and forums. For example, bloggers like Han Han and writers like Dangnian Mingyue produced high-quality content in China. It's hard to imagine today's Internet fostering serious discussions on democracy and freedom as it once did.

Tim Berners-Lee, the "Father of the Internet," believed the Internet's true value lay in granting equal access to information, helping humanity organize existing knowledge, and uncovering the unknown. He resisted any attempt to elitize the World Wide Web, erect barriers, or profit from it, embodying the spirit of decentralization.

Regrettably, the story followed a familiar pattern—technological advancements hoped to radically improve the human condition, yet often underscored inherent societal flaws. As digital technology evolved, shifting information dissemination from the centralized Web 1.0 to a self-media era with ubiquitous content creators and AI's growing control over information, humanity entered an age dominated by algorithms, ushering in a "post-truth" era.

1.3.2 The Shift from the Founding Vision in Web 2.0

As the Internet evolved into the Web 2.0 era, it began to stray from its foundational principles. O'Reilly Media, the proponent of the Web 2.0 concept, envisioned this era as transforming the Internet into a dynamic application platform, heralding a shift toward a more democratized network with widespread information sharing. The anticipation was that the Internet would bolster user empowerment through enhanced democratization.

Yet, as interactivity heightened, a shift in narrative emerged: the Internet's landscape expanded beyond individual users to encompass service providers, fostering spaces for user-generated content. At this juncture, platforms were largely perceived as benign enablers, providing essential infrastructure for democratizing the Internet through enriched interactive experiences.

Steve Krug's book *Don't Make Me Think* is often hailed as the "Bible" for Internet products and known in Chinese as "点石成金: 访客至上的网页设计秘笈," remains a staple recommendation for entrepreneurs, especially during the startup surge of 2015. It championed user convenience, suggesting that platforms should streamline user experiences.

However, the current landscape reveals a stark reality: Internet platforms have deeply penetrated our real lives. These platforms leverage user data, establish network effects, and dominate our digital existence. They harness our data for targeted advertising and, in some cases, have the potential to influence our perceptions and thoughts. This marked deviation from the Internet's original ethos underscores a pressing need to reassess and realign the direction of its evolution.

A prime example is the "Facebook data scandal" in March 2018. Personal data from 87 million Facebook users were sold to Cambridge Analytica, which manipulated the data to influence the Brexit vote and Trump's election.

Cambridge Analytica's "seed users" originated from a psychological test app on Facebook, which profiled individuals based on likes and social behaviors. The company claimed that with these profiles, they could accurately predict the behavior of the entire American population.

In April 2019, The *New York Times* published an article, "The Only Answer Is Less Internet," pushing mainstream media criticism of the Internet industry to new heights. That month alone, around 20 negative commentaries on the broader Internet industry appeared in major Western media.

By then, the Internet industry was no longer seen as a symbol of freedom and democracy but as a source of many societal ills. Despite their differences, the article argued that both Western and Eastern Internet models ultimately converged on centralization, diminishing citizen agency, infringing on privacy, and manipulating public opinion.

Examples abound, like social media platforms exercising control over user content, highlighting the limitations of online free speech, which relies on the platforms provided by Internet companies. These platforms are commercial and competitive, yet they wield significant power over user content, as seen in the actions of Weibo and WeChat in China and the banning of Donald Trump by Meta, X (Twitter), and YouTube during the 2020 US presidential election, illustrating the substantial control these platforms have over public discourse.

Interestingly, Trump was not just an individual; he represented a team with multiple Twitter accounts, such as his "TeamTrump" campaign account and the personal accounts of his campaign team's director. Trump attempted a "rebirth" through these accounts, but they were swiftly banned by the platform, which went as far as permanently banning accounts of Trump's team members like National Security Advisor Michael Flynn, lawyer Sidney Powell, and attorney Lin Wood. These accounts, all with millions of followers, were obliterated with a mere click on the platform.

Beyond account bans that directly interfere with citizens' freedom of expression, the filtering functions of Internet companies also limit online free speech. For market competition reasons, companies might choose to block or delete user comments detrimental to their growth or retain those that are aggressive toward competitors, thereby influencing users' attitudes and opinions.

Bot accounts, intelligent programs that mimic human user behavior on social networks, are becoming increasingly "realistic" with AI advancements. They can generate substantive content like images, videos, or texts and interact with users in authentic or fabricated ways. For instance, in 2017, researchers uncovered a vast zombie network on Twitter with over 350,000 bot accounts that had gone undetected since its inception in 2013. ZeroFOX revealed a massive spam porn botnet on Twitter, named "SIREN," comprising over 90,000 fake accounts that posted over 8.5 million tweets with malicious links.

Recent discussions in the Chinese Internet space have focused on the conflicts between food delivery riders and platforms. A 2020 report highlighted the precarious conditions in the delivery industry, where platforms continuously chase efficiency and cost reduction using big data and AI, pushing human limits by shortening delivery times and leading to numerous traffic accidents.

The intelligent dispatch system central to platform control over delivery riders further reinforces their dependency on the platform. This system, reliant on big data and AI, continually records and analyzes riders' data, assigning orders and monitoring their execution. Riders, stripped of autonomy and control over their time, must follow algorithmic instructions, a model that has led to increased traffic accidents involving delivery personnel.

The ideal of Web 2.0 has crumbled. While platforms facilitated easier Internet access and interaction from Web 1.0 to 2.0, they took more than they gave. Web 2.0 has ushered humanity from an era of limited truths to one devoid of absolute truths governed by platform algorithms.

With AI's advancement into true intelligence, exemplified by technologies like ChatGPT, AI can generate machine responses based on human requests in real-time, edging us toward an era dominated by machines. The emergence of tools like Sora challenges our civilization by transcending text to create videos or movies, the most accessible format for humans. Such content, indistinguishable in authenticity, artistry, and visual appeal to the untrained eye, can be generated in seconds and varied infinitely by AI.

This challenge is imminent as algorithms increasingly govern our society. Without adaptive changes, this algorithmic rule will deepen and expand, posing a profound challenge to human society.

1.3.3 Rebuilding Trust on the Internet

We must acknowledge that while the Internet is a remarkable technology, not all directions of its progress are beneficial. The dilemmas of Web 2.0 present an opportunity for the emergence of Web 3.0.

The core idea of Web 3.0 is to redesign current Internet services and products to benefit the public, not just corporate giants. Data will still drive decisions but won't be used to exploit consumers. Data rights will be protected, not just pursued for profit. Incentive and market mechanisms will help ensure the credibility and verifiability of information.

In Web 3.0, individual sovereignty is prioritized over the interests of the wealthy elite and rent-seekers. Individuals will have more control over their data and rights, and they will no longer be passively exploited. This means users will manage their digital footprint more autonomously, without concerns over misuse of personal information.

Web 3.0 emphasizes decentralization, aiming to eliminate the concentration of power in the traditional Internet. By employing blockchain technology and other means, Web 3.0 seeks to establish a distributed, transparent, and less manipulable network structure, reducing reliance on intermediaries and enhancing the network's stability and security.

Web 3.0 is not just about technology; it's about redefining the narrative of the Internet. We live not only in the Web 2.0 world but also under the Web 2.0 narrative that shapes our understanding of entrepreneurship, venerating concepts like the "Lean Principle," "rapid iteration," and the pursuit of "network effects," eventually epitomizing the "platform company" model. In this framework, data is the new oil, algorithmic recommendations become powerful content distribution tools, and "product manager thinking" is encouraged in every employee.

This "Internet thinking" narrative has indeed achieved success to some extent. Entrepreneurs chase "network effects," developers value "rapid iteration," and data supremacy is an unquestionable doctrine in the Internet realm. This mindset has driven rapid technological progress and innovation, cultivating a generation of data-oriented entrepreneurs and professionals.

However, this narrative has its downsides. An excessive focus on "network effects" can lead to monopolies, restricting competition and innovation. Blind pursuit of "rapid iteration" may overlook product quality and sustainable development, leading to shortsighted decisions. The data supremacy doctrine can raise privacy and security concerns, causing societal apprehension.

The emergence of Web 3.0 challenges this narrative. It represents a profound reflection on "Internet thinking," prompting those accustomed to the Web 2.0 narrative to question its correctness. It encourages a reevaluation of accepted norms: Does the Internet necessarily need to pursue network effects? Are becoming a platform company or allying with one the only options for Internet companies? Should users only have usage rights without ownership? Is more data always better, and for whom?

As the Web 2.0 narrative fractures, new Internet philosophies emerge. By reexamining familiar concepts, our imagination of the Internet is rekindled. The narrative under Web 3.0 is a revolution against Web 2.0, signifying not just an upgrade but a fundamentally different concept, an inevitability in advancing AI, computing, and communication technologies. Web 3.0 is not solely a technical issue but a broader question shaped by ideology and technology, focusing on building a better Internet. Technology is merely a means; our core focus should be the values and principles we hold for the Internet.

Often, it's only when technology encounters issues that we genuinely contemplate the problems we need technology to solve. We continually discover and address issues within technology, sparking new technological advancements. The value prioritization in addressing these issues is itself an ideological matter. Technological progress leads to ideological shifts, which in turn drive further technological advancement, creating a cycle. A new cycle has begun, heralding a new Internet paradigm.

Perhaps this signifies our ongoing exploration as a society. We constantly invent new technologies, which in turn breed new challenges, prompting us to seek new solutions, thus propelling humanity forward in an endless cycle. We are both the creators and solvers of problems, navigating the uncharted territories of human progress.

CHAPTER 2

The Infrastructure of Web 3.0

2.1 Blockchain: The Core Technology of Web 3.0

Although Web 3.0 is widely regarded as the next generation of the Internet, there's still no unified understanding or definition of Web 3.0 in academia or the business world. However, the consensus is clear: blockchain is the core supporting technology of Web 3.0.

2.1.1 Blockchain = Block + Chain

Blockchain stands as a seminal innovation in the annals of scientific and technological progress. In 2008, an individual or group under the pseudonym Satoshi Nakamoto introduced blockchain through the paper "Bitcoin: A Peer-to-Peer Electronic Cash System," leveraging Bitcoin to elucidate this then-nascent concept. Initially met with skepticism, blockchain technology has, over the years, not only ignited a transformative wave across the banking and finance sectors but also established itself as a cutting-edge technology in the realms of data computation and storage.

Globally recognized, blockchain is delineated as a peer-to-peer network framework employing cryptographic methods and consensus protocols, among other technologies, to generate and maintain an extensive sequence of transactional data blocks. Each block is secured with the cryptographic hash of its predecessor, timestamped, and bundled with transaction data, thereby rendering any retroactive alterations to the block's contents a formidable challenge.

At its core, blockchain serves as a decentralized ledger, facilitating transactions between mutually distrusting entities without the requisite of a centralized authority. This groundbreaking mode leverages a suite of computer technologies, including distributed data storage, peer-to-peer transmission, consensus mechanisms, and cryptographic algorithms, emblematic of the digital age. The paramount deployment of blockchain is epitomized in cryptocurrencies like Bitcoin, where the fundamental transactional operation entails debiting an amount from one account and crediting it to another. With a universally accessible ledger chronicling every transaction heretofore, the extant balance of any given account can be ascertained. In essence, blockchain has transitioned the accounting paradigm from a solitary keeper to a communal endeavor, significantly bolstering the integrity and security of transactional records.

Blockchain's architecture is bifurcated into two segments: "block" and "chain," which collectively articulate the technology's data configuration. A block represents a data segment, meticulously crafted through cryptographic techniques and preserved perpetually as electronic records within a "block." Each block meticulously documents various elements, encompassing a nonce, block size, block header information, transaction count, and detailed transaction data. Structurally, a block is composed of a block header and a block body—the header maintains a linkage to the preceding block's address, ensuring the blockchain database's integrity, while the block body harbors the authenticated transaction details or alternative data records.

The integrity and precision of blockchain data are safeguarded via two pivotal mechanisms: First, each block chronicles the transactions transpiring post the formation of the preceding block and prior to the current block's creation, thus guaranteeing the database's completeness. Second, once a block is annexed to the blockchain, its data entries become immutable, reinforcing the database's precision.

The chain's anatomy is predicated on the interconnection of blocks via their headers, with each header recording the hash values of both the preceding and the current block, thereby interlinking all blocks into a coherent information sequence.

Temporal markers on blocks introduce a chronological dimension to the blockchain. The older blocks, bearing more subsequent block linkages, become progressively challenging to modify. Blocks employ cryptographic protocols, facilitating a network of computers (nodes) to collaboratively maintain a shared distributed ledger, even in the absence of absolute trust amongst nodes.

This framework ensures that, provided the majority of the network adheres to the block publication rules, the information encapsulated within the blockchain is deemed reliable. It assures a uniform replication of transaction data throughout the network. With the presence of a distributed storage mechanism, all network nodes characteristically possess the entirety of the information stored on the blockchain, mirroring the earth's crust—wherein deeper layers (older blocks) epitomize increased stability and immutability.

Given that all transactions from the genesis block are recorded in plaintext on the blockchain and are immutable, any value exchanges between transaction participants are traceable and queryable. This transparent data management paradigm is not only legally robust but also furnishes a trustworthy avenue for logistics tracking, operational log documentation, auditing, and account verification.

Occasionally, blockchain encounters "forks" instances where two qualifying blocks emerge simultaneously. Fork resolution entails extending the timeline, awaiting the subsequent block, and annexing the lengthier branch to the primary chain. Forks are anomalous, with the likelihood of multiple forks being infinitesimal. A fork represents a transient state, with the blockchain ultimately converging toward a singular, longest chain.

From a regulatory and audit perspective, entries can be appended to the distributed ledger but not excised. A consortium of communication nodes operating bespoke software collectively replicates and sustains the distributed ledger in a peer-to-peer modality. All information propagated on the blockchain is auditable, bearing a traceable digital "fingerprint." The ledger's data is universally accessible and enduring, engendering a dependable "transaction cloud" that mitigates data loss, thereby inherently obliterating counterparty risks and data discrepancies in inter-party transactions.

2.1.2 Web 3.0 Needs Blockchain

A central vision for Web 3.0 is "decentralization," which is in perfect harmony with the inherent strengths of blockchain technology. While Web 2.0, with its client-server architecture or cloud computing frameworks, operates on a centralized model, the rise of Web 3.0 seeks to address the evolving challenges and limitations inherent in Web 2.0's structure.

Issues such as security vulnerabilities have become increasingly acute in our interconnected Web 2.0 world. With copious amounts of personal data stored on centralized servers, these repositories become prime targets for cyber-attacks, risking data breaches, identity theft, and the introduction of malicious software. Privacy is another pressing concern in Web 2.0, where user data is typically held and managed by third-party entities, stripping users of control over their own information. Moreover, the authenticity of information shared across platforms like social media is often questionable, leading to the proliferation of misinformation, thereby eroding trust and integrity in digital communications.

Contrastingly, blockchain introduces a pioneering distributed framework and computing philosophy that champions openness and democratization. Utilizing blockchain data structures, distributed node consensus algorithms, and advanced cryptographic methods, blockchain shifts the trajectory of the Internet toward greater transparency and equality.

The blockchain structure itself—a sequence of data blocks containing transactional records linked in a chain—embodies immutability, ensuring that once data is entered, it is secure and unalterable. Distributed consensus algorithms across network nodes collaborate to authenticate transactions, eliminating central points of failure and bolstering the system's resilience. Cryptographic methods ensure data is securely transmitted and stored, enhancing user privacy and data security.

These foundational elements of blockchain culminate in its pivotal feature: decentralization. Data is not hoarded in a singular location but is dispersed across numerous network nodes, democratizing control and ownership.

This decentralized model empowers users to manage their digital assets and personal data without reliance on third-party mediators. It fosters direct, peer-to-peer interactions, streamlining and securing exchanges. Moreover, the decentralized nature of blockchain mitigates risks of data manipulation and enhances system reliability—even if some nodes are compromised, the network at large remains operational.

Crucially, blockchain technology confronts the centralization and data control issues endemic to Web 2.0. Rather than users placing trust in platforms to safeguard their data—often leading to privacy violations and data misuse—Web 3.0, powered by blockchain, distributes data across a network, placing control back in users' hands. For instance, in a blockchain-based social media platform, user data is encrypted and decentralized, enabling individuals to maintain data sovereignty even amid platform compromises or closures.

In the contemporary technological paradigm, the transition to Web 3.0 inherently necessitates embracing blockchain as a foundational technology, marking a significant step toward a more decentralized, secure, and user-empowered digital landscape.

2.2 Smart Contracts: Facilitating Trustworthy Transactions in Web 3.0

In the digital age, social and economic activities on the Internet inevitably involve interactions and collaborations. During the Web 1.0 and Web 2.0 eras, facilitating cooperation among strangers in a virtual environment posed significant challenges. Traditionally, these interactions relied on intermediary platforms to mediate and secure cooperation, leading to various trust, security, and efficiency issues.

However, the advent of Web 3.0 and the emergence of blockchain technology introduce a groundbreaking approach to collaboration: smart contracts. These blockchain-enabled contracts infuse digital social and economic interactions with enhanced trust, transparency, and decentralization, offering a novel paradigm for Internet-based cooperation.

2.2.1 From Bitcoin to Ethereum

Blockchain technology, from its inception as Blockchain 1.0 to the current Blockchain 3.0, has entered an era of profound exploration and development. Among its pivotal contributions, the two most significant native applications of blockchain are the distributed ledger, which has revolutionized digital currency, and smart contracts.

Originally, Blockchain 1.0 referred exclusively to Bitcoin's ledger, which chronicled all transactions from the network's beginning. Viewed as a secure global ledger, blockchain ensured that all digitally transactable activities were indelibly recorded.

Satoshi Nakamoto, the enigmatic creator of Bitcoin, unveiled a paper titled "Bitcoin: A Peer-to-Peer Electronic Cash System" on October 31, 2008. Nakamoto introduced a new electronic currency system designed to operate independently of governmental or institutional oversight. This system, underpinned by decentralization, non-inflation, and infinite divisibility, established blockchain technology as the bedrock of Bitcoin's functionality.

In January 2009, Nakamoto released Bitcoin's open-source software on SourceForge and mined the inaugural 50 bitcoins, marking the genesis block's creation. Shortly after, Nakamoto facilitated Bitcoin's first transaction by sending ten bitcoins to cryptographer Hal Finney, signaling the commencement of an unstoppable Bitcoin movement.

By 2010, the first Bitcoin exchange emerged, and Bitcoin began to gain market traction, though initially limited to tech enthusiasts. These early adopters mined, discussed, and traded Bitcoin, nurturing the fledgling community.

Bitcoin exemplified decentralized ledger technology, where a network of participants maintained a consistent ledger, deciding account-keeping rights through computational "mining." This decentralized, secure, and immutable ledger, incentivized by mining rewards, has, over a decade, garnered recognition from global institutions and governments as a viable store of value.

Following Bitcoin's trailblazing path, Ethereum emerged, enhancing blockchain's capabilities to support sophisticated program logic and smart contracts, transitioning from a mere decentralized ledger (Blockchain 1.0) to a comprehensive decentralized computing platform (Blockchain 2.0).

Ethereum, conceived by Vitalik Buterin in late 2013, represented the dawn of a dynamic digital token ecosystem. Envisioned as blockchain's "Android system," Ethereum empowered developers to craft applications within its framework, spawning a myriad of blockchain-based innovations.

The notion of smart contracts, though proposed by Nick Szabo in 1994, found practical application with Ethereum. Szabo envisioned smart contracts as transaction protocols that autonomously execute contract terms, potentially obviating the need for intermediaries. Ethereum's introduction of Turing-complete scripting capabilities transformed it into a "world computer," where developers could craft an array of smart contracts and dApps.

Through Ethereum's smart contracts and virtual machines, decentralized computing was realized, enabling the creation and deployment of varied dApps and contracts. Miners executed these smart contracts, validated them across the network, and ensured the integrity and trustworthiness of the computational results.

Public and transparent, Ethereum's smart contracts support mutual invocation, fostering an ecosystem characterized by openness and trust. Essentially, Ethereum encodes agreements into programmable "If-else" statements, facilitating automatic execution upon condition fulfillment, thus minimizing the friction and costs associated with traditional verification and enforcement mechanisms.

2.2.2 Smart Contracts: The Backbone of Web 3.0 Transactions

"Contract" is a legally binding agreement established among several free individuals, a concept of significant weight throughout human societal development. Jean-Jacques Rousseau's *The Social Contract*, revered as the bible by all factions of the French Revolution, posits that an ideal society is built on contractual relationships among individuals, essentially framing contracts as the foundation of modern social civilization. The Napoleonic Code of 1804 preliminarily established the principle of "freedom of contract" as a fundamental principle of all contemporary civil law. Today, the contemporary social order and legal system in which most of the world's population lives are constructed on this foundational concept of "contract."

This cherished principle of "freedom of contract" is technically embodied in the blockchain's feature of "decentralization," with smart contracts being a direct application of this blockchain technology in Web 3.0. These digital contracts automate agreements between parties directly within the code. Unlike traditional contracts, which require physical signatures and often third-party enforcement, smart contracts execute automatically when predefined conditions are met, without the need for intermediary oversight or manual intervention.

Consider a rental agreement between a landlord and a tenant. Traditionally, this involves signing a physical document and often an intermediary to enforce the contract's terms. In the Web 3.0 context, a smart contract could streamline this entire process. The contract's terms are coded into the blockchain, allowing for automatic rent transfer from the tenant to the landlord, concurrent with the digital handover of property access codes, exemplifying how smart contracts can eliminate intermediary costs and enhance transaction efficiency.

The pivotal role of smart contracts in Web 3.0 extends beyond simplifying transactions; it revolutionizes the underlying trust mechanism in digital cooperation. Where traditional contracts depend on legal frameworks or intermediaries for enforcement, smart contracts, with their code-defined rules, ensure automatic execution, fostering direct and efficient interaction among parties.

Decentralization is another cornerstone of smart contracts, enhancing trust and reducing collaboration risks by distributing contract execution across the network rather than depending on a single centralized authority. This not only diminishes reliance on intermediaries but also mitigates single points of failure, ensuring that the contract terms remain unaltered and execution outcomes can be trusted without fear of manipulation.

Additionally, smart contracts streamline transaction processes, reducing costs associated with intermediaries and manual processing, thereby reflecting economic efficiency directly in transactions. As a quintessential technology of Web 3.0, smart contracts pave the way for novel business models, transforming traditional commerce and propelling digital economy innovation.

Smart contracts decentralize traditional commerce, allowing for fair and transparent trade without the oversight of centralized authorities, thus enhancing the credibility and fairness of the business ecosystem. Their automated execution accelerates business activities, lowers costs, and encourages business model innovation by providing a flexible framework free from the constraints of centralized institutions.

In summary, smart contracts in Web 3.0 are not merely a technological evolution but a paradigm shift in business cooperation, fostering a digital economy that is more efficient, transparent, and inclusive, and setting a robust foundation for the digital society's future.

2.2.3 Smart Contracts Today

Smart contracts have found application across a broad spectrum of scenarios, with Ethereum emerging as a prime platform for their deployment. Ethereum's comprehensive smart contract programming capabilities and development tools empower creators to build a variety of dApps. These dApps leverage smart contracts to decentralize crucial operations, addressing trust issues in scenarios ranging from financial transactions to value assignments in gaming. Unlike conventional web applications, dApps eliminate the need for user registration, identifying participants through decentralized addresses.

Decentralized finance (DeFi) stands out as a vibrant domain within dApps, reimagining financial contracts through smart contracts to deliver a spectrum of decentralized financial services. DeFi reconstitutes traditional financial systems on the blockchain, encoding financial contracts to enable direct user involvement in activities like lending or utilizing digital assets as collateral. Transactions and repayments are autonomously managed by smart contracts, dispensing with the reliance on intermediaries. This decentralized approach to finance enhances accessibility, transparency, and inclusivity in financial services.

In the context of the forthcoming Web 3.0 era, DeFi empowers users with full control over their assets on the blockchain, contrasting with traditional financial systems where assets are typically under centralized institutional control. DeFi's use of blockchain and smart contracts affords users direct asset management and autonomy, diminishing dependency on conventional financial entities and reducing associated trust risks.

Moreover, DeFi overcomes geographical limitations and trust barriers inherent in traditional finance, facilitating global financial participation without regional constraints. Smart contracts' automatic execution feature minimizes the need for intermediary trust, mitigating opaque operations prevalent in traditional finance and fostering transparency and fairness in financial transactions.

The convergence of DeFi and NFTs expands Web 3.0's application scope. Merging DeFi's financial mechanics with the unique properties of NFTs enables applications to span content, intellectual property, records, and identity verification in Web 3.0. For instance, NFTs can represent unique digital artwork ownership, while DeFi offers financial mechanisms for trading and investing in digital art. This synergy fosters a transparent and autonomous financial ecosystem, accommodating diverse assets and facilitating complex transactions, which is pivotal for Web 3.0's infrastructure.

Furthermore, smart contracts are instrumental in establishing a secure and reliable digital identity framework. They manage personal identity information (PII), ensuring only authorized access, enhancing privacy protection, and mitigating risks linked to centralized data repositories.

These applications represent just a fraction of the potential smart contracts harbor. In essence, the emergence of smart contracts is integral to Web 3.0's evolution. They enable decentralized, secure, and efficient transaction methods, catalyzing new business models and reshaping social organizations for the Web 3.0 landscape.

2.3 NFTs: The Carriers of Rights in Web 3.0

Tokens function as the foundational units within blockchain-based frameworks, serving as the elemental components of Web 3.0. These tokens encapsulate a user's rights and status on the Internet, allowing individuals to acquire and exercise specific online rights and privileges through the possession and exchange of these tokens. Additionally, tokens can embody digital assets, symbolizing tangible properties or rights, and heralding an innovative trajectory for the digital economy's progression.

In the Web 3.0 epoch, the authentication and management of digital rights necessitate the tokenization of users' online identities, encapsulating their status via tokens. This process of tokenization can be safeguarded through smart contracts on the blockchain, ensuring the rights' transparency and immutability.

NFTs, a distinct subset of tokens, are pivotal within the Web 3.0 ecosystem. NFTs empower users to engage in the digital economy, validate the authenticity of digital assets, and acquire rewards, all within a decentralized blockchain framework. These unique tokens offer a mechanism for validating ownership and provenance of digital items, enabling creators and users alike to transact and interact in an authenticated and secure digital landscape.

2.3.1 The Technical Essence of NFTs

Technologically, NFTs are an advanced application born from the further technical and applicative development of blockchain technology, an inevitable evolution.

As previously discussed, Bitcoin in the Blockchain 1.0 era established a decentralized system for record-keeping and transactions. Its value storage function has gained acceptance among various global institutions and governments over a decade. Bitcoin's success demonstrates the effective realization of decentralized value transfer. Building upon Bitcoin's foundation, Ethereum introduced an upgrade, supporting complex program logic and giving birth to smart contracts. Currently, dApps based on smart contracts are flourishing in finance, gaming, and social networking, with a steady increase in user and asset numbers.

As dApps expand, the inevitable surge in distributed data necessitates unique identifiers. For these distributed data to engage in transactions, detailed and secure identifiers are essential. This necessity gives rise to NFT technology.

NFTs originated from the 2017 blockchain game *CryptoKitties*. They provided a fresh perspective on addressing copyright issues—once a work is tokenized and put on the blockchain, it gains an immutable, unique code. This ensures that, despite numerous copies or distributions, the original creator retains sole ownership.

In contrast to fungible tokens like Bitcoin, every NFT is unique and indivisible, forming the core value of NFTs. Supported by blockchain, even if an NFT work is downloaded or captured by others, the original owner can prove the work's authenticity through digital certificates or other means. It's analogous to how numerous replicas of the *Mona Lisa* exist in the art market, but the original remains unique in the Louvre.

The advantages of NFTs are clear. They offer a digital "key," with each NFT's rarity and irreplaceability backed by blockchain, ensuring the authenticity of ownership and copyright. This aligns with traditional supply-demand principles, facilitating the transfer and exercise of rights for purchasers. Furthermore, various associated permissions can exist outside centralized services or databases. This significantly enhances the efficiency of data asset transactions and accelerates digital asset trends. Previously, digital items like game equipment or virtual gifts stored on service provider servers didn't truly belong to players, posing risks of damage, theft, or illicit trading. However, blockchain allows developers to create and assure the rarity of virtual items, enabling users to securely and reliably save and trade their possessions.

Whether from a technical essence or the future development of Web 3.0, NFTs are a clear trend. In the short term, NFTs mainly digitalize and transact virtual properties represented by artworks. In the medium term, traditional assets like stocks or private equity will go on-chain, enabling liquidity conversion. In the long run, with systems like oracles, the transition from asset Internetization to on-chain assets will occur, bearing richer asset values.

In essence, NFTs are the tagging technology in the digital world. Evidently, every character in the digital realm is backed by specific codes. By tagging these codes, we create what's known as NFTs today.

2.3.2 Understanding NFT

In today's digital landscape, NFTs are reshaping the concept of ownership and rights within the burgeoning Web 3.0 ecosystem. NFTs, as unique digital assets, are revolutionizing how we perceive and engage with digital content, offering a secure, transparent method to claim ownership over a myriad of virtual goods—from digital art to in-game items.

NFTs are transforming the collectibles market, providing a digital form of scarcity that is ideally suited for collectibles whose value is intrinsically linked to their limited availability. Pioneering implementations of NFTs in the collectibles space, such as Crypto Kitties and Crypto Punks, underscored their potential, with certain Crypto Punks fetching millions in auctions. The advent of NFTs in platforms like NBA TopShot, which immortalizes NBA highlights as collectible NFTs, illustrates the expanding horizon of NFT applications beyond mere static images.

In the realm of art, NFTs empower artists to sell their creations directly in digital format, circumventing the need to transmute their artworks into physical objects. This paradigm shift not only ensures artists benefit from initial sales but also allows them to partake in the proceeds of secondary market transactions, fostering a more equitable ecosystem for creators. The rise of dedicated NFT art marketplaces, such as Nifty Gateway 7, highlights the growing acceptance and valuation of digital art, with sales reaching astronomical figures.

Within the gaming industry, NFTs introduce a groundbreaking concept of asset ownership, enabling players to truly own, earn, and trade their in-game assets across platforms and marketplaces, a stark departure from traditional gaming models where users' investments in digital assets remain confined within specific game environments.

Moreover, NFTs are set to redefine the business model of virtual goods, transforming these goods from mere services to tradable entities. Traditional virtual goods, characterized by their infinite replicability and negligible production costs, are typically sold as services. NFTs disrupt this model, allowing creators to mint and trade virtual goods as unique, verifiable assets, thereby enhancing the value and utility of digital creations.

For Web 3.0, NFTs are not just a technological innovation but a cornerstone of the decentralized economy. They facilitate autonomous, direct peer-to-peer transactions and collaborations, mediated by smart contracts, eliminating the need for centralized intermediaries. This shift heralds a more democratic, open, and efficient economic landscape, promising to spur continued innovation and growth in the digital economy.

As we venture deeper into the Web 3.0 era, NFTs stand as a testament to the evolving relationship between technology and ownership, redefining rights, transactions, and interactions in the digital realm. Their integration into various sectors underscores their versatility and potential to catalyze a profound transformation in how we conceive and interact with digital assets.

2.4 Decentralized Autonomous Organization (DAO): The Organizational Paradigm of Web 3.0

The advent of Web 3.0 demands not just innovative technologies, contract methodologies, and mechanisms for asset representation but also necessitates a reimagining of organizational structures. This is where DAO comes into play, embodying the organizational archetype for the Web 3.0 epoch.

DAOs are emblematic of the blockchain ethos—emphasizing co-creation, joint governance, and shared benefits. These entities operate on a decentralized framework, diverging from traditional, centralized governance models. The essence of a DAO is its community-centric approach, where hierarchical management is supplanted by collective autonomy and where the traditional corporate backbone is replaced by self-regulating communities.

A DAO facilitates a collaborative environment where individuals worldwide, despite not knowing each other, can converge on a shared platform to make collective decisions within a predefined rule set and share the outcomes of these decisions. This model aligns seamlessly with the vision of Web 3.0, where collaboration, transparency, and decentralization are pivotal.

2.4.1 The Origin of DAO

From the Internet's early days, a pressing question has been how to enable the free exchange of value in an environment lacking mutual trust. Blockchain technology has emerged as a premier answer to this dilemma. But the inquiry extends further: can individuals with shared goals come together to collaborate, work, or fulfill tasks in a manner that's both secure and efficient? This question has given rise to the concept of DAOs.

In 2006, science fiction author Daniel Suarez published *Daemon*, a book that can be considered an early text on DAOs. *Daemon* describes a computer application that, based on distributed characteristics, secretly takes over hundreds of companies to establish a new world order. The operation of the Daemon mirrors today's DAOs: offering bounties, sharing information across the community, and managing currency.

While similar in function, "Daemon" did not directly coin the term "DAO." The actual birth of DAOs traces back to 2013 when Invictus Innovations CEO Daniel Larimer first proposed the concept of DAC (Decentralized Autonomous Corporation). He saw DAC as an effective metaphor for decentralized systems providing useful goods and services to society, playing efficient roles in various fields such as news aggregation, AdWords, domain names, patents, copyrights, next-generation intellectual property, insurance, courts, escrow and arbitration, anonymous voting authorization, prediction markets, and next-generation search engines. Larimer emphasized that DACs should operate on their blockchain for exchanging shares, must not rely on any individual, company, or organization to possess value, should not own private keys, and must not depend on any legal contracts. Vitalik Buterin later introduced DAOs, distinguishing them from DACs by noting that DACs, which introduce the concept of shares, are for-profit entities, whereas he emphasized that DAOs should be nonprofit entities, even though they can profit by participating in their ecosystem.

In 2014, Vitalik published "DAOs, DACs, DAs, and More: An Incomplete Terminology Guide," further detailing the potential for organizational governance based on blockchain technology. In 2016, "The DAO," the world's first and most famous DAO, was launched on the Ethereum blockchain. It started with a visionary goal: to become a venture fund for the Ethereum community, managed in a decentralized manner, with members crowdfunding into The DAO and voting collectively on investments via tokens.

"The DAO" quickly raised 12.7 million ETH, equivalent to $150 million at the time, with over 11,000 participants. However, it soon encountered significant setbacks due to a technical flaw in its smart contract code, leading to a controversial hard fork in the Ethereum blockchain, resulting in Ethereum and Ethereum Classic.

However, The DAO did not develop as smoothly as expected and soon experienced significant setbacks. In June of the same year, The DAO encountered a technical flaw in its smart contract code, allowing hackers to steal over $50 million worth of ETH. This incident led to a controversial hard fork in the Ethereum blockchain, resulting in two separate chains: Ethereum and Ethereum Classic.

Despite the issues faced by The DAO, the concept of DAOs did not come to a halt. Particularly, the initiative by MolochDAO, created in January 2019, acted as a catalyst for the rebirth of DAOs. The core innovation of MolochDAO was the introduction of the ERC-20 standard for DAO smart contracts, which sparked the creation of a series of new DAOs as its direct offshoots. Today, thousands of DAOs operate across various blockchain networks, including Ethereum, EOS, and Tezos. DAOs are utilized in various sectors, from DeFi to supply chain management and social media platforms. The concept of DAOs continues to evolve, and we are likely to see ongoing innovation and growth in this area in the coming years.

2.4.2 Dissecting the Concept of DAO

Despite the increasing visibility of DAOs, a clear understanding of what precisely constitutes a DAO remains essential. As defined by Wikipedia, a DAO is an organization embodied in transparent computer code, managed by organization members, and not influenced by any central government. The financial transactions and programmatic rules of a DAO are maintained on a blockchain.

At its core, the notion of the DAO isn't entirely novel. What distinguishes DAOs from earlier forms of decentralized entities is their governance and operations through blockchain-enabled smart contracts. In a DAO, governance rules are encoded within the blockchain via program code, ensuring that the organization's governance, operations, and transactions are conducted via smart contracts.

Breaking down the concept reveals two fundamental aspects: decentralization and autonomy.

Decentralization in the context of DAOs refers to an organizational design principle that eschews reliance on a single central authority. Instead, it distributes power and control across a network of nodes. While traditional centralized entities consolidate power and control, often leading to issues like opacity in decision-making and vulnerability to single points of failure, decentralization disperses power across various nodes, enhancing transparency, resilience, and fairness.

In DAOs, decentralization is more than a principle; it's a practice. Governance and operational protocols are not under the purview of a single entity but are shared among members through the blockchain. This approach ensures that all members have an equitable stake in decision-making processes, promoting fairness and collective responsibility.

Autonomy within DAOs refers to the self-governing capacity of the organization, where decision-making and rule enforcement are carried out by members autonomously, without external intervention. Traditional organizations often rely on hierarchical decision-making, which can be inefficient and inflexible. Conversely, DAOs leverage smart contracts to automate rule execution, ensuring decisions are enacted swiftly and accurately, reducing the potential for human error or manipulation.

This autonomous framework empowers members to directly influence the organization's trajectory through democratic processes like voting. The execution of these decisions, facilitated by smart contracts, underscores the organization's self-sustaining nature. It ensures that the organization remains nimble, adaptable, and aligned with the collective will of its members.

In summary, the exploration of DAOs reveals a paradigm where decentralization and autonomy converge to create a new form of organizational structure. This structure is not only robust and transparent but also inherently democratic, aligning closely with the foundational principles of the Web 3.0 era.

DAOs present a transformative approach to organization and governance, offering several distinct advantages over traditional organizational structures:

(1) Democratic governance. DAOs operate on a principle of collective governance, eliminating traditional hierarchical structures. Every member has a say in decision-making processes, usually through a voting system, ensuring a democratic environment where decisions are not monopolized by a few individuals but are the result of collective agreement.

(2) Task-driven and participant-centric. The essence of DAOs is task-driven value creation, where participants choose and engage in projects that resonate with them. Unlike traditional organizational structures where employees might feel disconnected, DAO participants are actively involved and motivated by both financial rewards and a sense of fulfillment and purpose in their contributions.

(3) Inclusive decision-making. DAOs foster an environment where every member's voice matters. Decisions are made based on votes, with each member's influence often tied to their token holdings. This system ensures that decisions are made transparently and inclusively, reflecting the collective will of the participants.

(4) Transparency and automation. Leveraging blockchain technology and smart contracts, DAOs operate with a level of transparency and automation not found in traditional organizations. Every action and decision is recorded on the blockchain, visible to all members, reducing the potential for

corruption and ensuring that contributions are fairly rewarded through automated processes.

The rise of DAOs is particularly resonant with the ethos of Web 3.0, which emphasizes decentralization and user empowerment. While Web 2.0 saw the centralization of power and information, leading to issues like data misuse and lack of transparency, Web 3.0 seeks to distribute power more equitably through decentralized technologies.

In this new digital era, DAOs represent a significant shift toward a more participatory, transparent, and equitable model of organization and governance, aligning with Web 3.0's vision of a more interconnected, user-centric online world. As digital technologies continue to evolve, DAOs stand as a beacon of how collaboration and community can be reimagined, paving the way for a future where power and decision-making are more widely distributed and aligned with the collective interests of all participants.

2.4.3 Types of DAOs

Just as there are diverse types of organizations in today's landscape, DAOs also manifest in various forms. Broadly speaking, most DAOs can be categorized as either technically oriented or socially oriented. Technically oriented DAOs tend to focus on construction within the cryptocurrency domain, often engaging more in blockchain-based operations. In contrast, socially oriented DAOs aim to unify individuals, exploring new methods of interaction and community building. In these DAOs, the "governance" process may not necessarily be blockchain-based or even require governance at all.

However, there isn't a stark boundary between different types of DAOs. Like the spectrum of "decentralization-autonomy," DAOs often exist somewhere between technical and social orientations, with many subcategories warranting individual attention:

(1) Protocol DAOs. Protocol DAOs are collaborative entities designed to aid protocol construction. A prime example is MakerDAO, which is not built or managed by a centralized team but rather by a series of interconnected DAOs. Over years of operation, MakerDAO has developed a complex structure consisting of 15 core units, each with specific tasks and budgets, managed by one or more coordinators who organize and reward contributors, driving toward MakerDAO's long-term objectives. Furthermore, each department within MakerDAO operates independently and is governed by its own set of terms while still being responsive to Maker token holders. Other examples like Sushi, Uniswap, and Compound can also be considered as protocol DAOs, although each operates according to its unique structure.

(2) Social DAOs. Friends with Benefits (FWB) is a notable example of a social DAO, which, while still following the principle of "birds of a feather flock together," coordinates its community mechanisms through tokens. For instance, to join FWB, users must apply and send 75 FWB tokens. These tokens can be viewed as a measure of contribution or a form of earnest money (membership fee). Once accepted, users join a community buzzing with developers, artists, and creators. This token-based coordination mechanism fosters a valuable community, with the token's value appreciating as more people join. Seed Club, founded by Jess Sloss, and others like CabinDAO and Bright Moments, also fall under the social DAO category.

(3) Creator DAOs. Centered around individual creators, creator DAOs are akin to fan clubs, providing support and interaction opportunities for their most influential supporters. While not widespread yet, many creators are beginning to leverage social tokens on platforms like Roll to meet these needs, paving the way for the growth of true creator DAOs.

(4) Investor DAOs. If social DAOs are about community, investor DAOs focus on returns. Unlike traditional venture capital, decisions in investor DAOs are genuinely democratic, made by limited partners through voting on investment choices. Each investor DAO might have a specific focus, such as specializing in purchasing ENS names, concentrating on blockchain games, or investing in crypto startups. LAO, established by Aaron Wright, exemplifies this category, giving rise to several other investment DAOs like Flamingo and Neptune. MetaCartel is another noteworthy investor DAO.

(5) Collector DAOs. Similar to investor DAOs in their profit-driven nature, collector DAOs have a distinct focus, organizing contributors around specific assets or collections, often deciding collectively on acquiring art pieces or other digital assets. NFTs are a common choice. While NFT accumulation can lead to substantial financial returns, these DAOs typically do not intend to sell their collections, at least in the short to medium term. Beyond investment, collector DAOs' involvement in NFTs often stems from a genuine appreciation of art. Besides collecting, collector DAOs sometimes play a role in conceptualizing NFT projects, lending institutional endorsement and support. Examples include SquiggleDAO, PleasrDAO, and NounsDAO, each with its unique functionality and organizational approach.

For instance, PleasrDAO, initiated by a group of early NFT collectors and digital artists, was established with the primary goal of raising funds to purchase NFT artworks. It gained prominence with its acquisition of an animation NFT for Uniswap V3, created by the artist Pplpleasr, for 310 ETH. PleasrDAO evolved to focus not just on acquiring artworks by Pplpleasr but also on collecting intriguing and valuable NFT artworks more broadly. A significant innovation brought by PleasrDAO is the unique mechanism of fractionalized ownership of NFTs, allowing collective possession of high-value art pieces, which opens new dimensions for the collection and management of NFT artworks.

In this evolving trend, traditional double-entry bookkeeping may soon transition to distributed ledger technology. This ledger extends beyond financial records to encompass all measurable efforts. Subsequently, laws protecting private and even public assets could evolve into smart contracts. Various tangible and intangible assets, along with their owner-ship, transfers, exchanges, and other related activities, are clearly arranged within smart contracts. Ultimately, companies, associations, and familiar organizational structures may gradually transform into DAOs.

At its core, the underlying philosophy of DAOs is "collective wisdom." The ancient Chinese philosopher Wenzi emphasized the power of the collective during the Spring and Autumn and Warring States periods, stating, "Where collective strength is applied, there is no failure; where collective wisdom is employed, there is no unachieved success." He repeatedly underscored the importance of collective effort in his writings. This notion resonates with Western philosophy, where Aristotle believed that a synthesis of multiple individuals' wisdom could yield superior conclusions compared to relying on a single expert.

Hence, we shouldn't overemphasize the term DAO. It serves more as a symbol of our vision for a decentralized Web 3.0, grounded in the concept of digital sovereignty and ideals of equality and freedom. The longevity of the term DAO, or its replacement by a new term, remains uncertain at present. However, it's foreseeable that the term DAO and the concepts it embodies will manifest in new forms within the true era of Web 3.0.

From collective wisdom and co-creation to shared enjoyment, the future of Web 3.0 is gradually unfolding.

—CHAPTER 3—

Industrial Applications of Web 3.0

3.1 Social Interaction in Web 3.0

Social interaction, one of humanity's most primal needs, serves as a means of connecting people and, in turn, drives the circulation of information, resources, and goods. The significance and universality of social interaction are self-evident. Due to its immense potential and value, social products have always captured the imagination of the capital market, with various blockchain ecosystems competing to develop or embrace social platforms.

In the current era of Web 2.0, characterized by frequent data breaches, privacy controversies, and algorithmic biases, social interaction in Web 3.0 has emerged as a new focal point for society and the capital market.

3.1.1 The Evolution of Social Forms

Social interaction, a fundamental human need, has evolved through various forms and means of communication. From ancient letters and coffee houses to modern social networks, the essence of social media has not changed; only its forms and technological tools have evolved.

In ancient times, letters and postal systems were the primary means of social interaction. With the invention of the printing press, books and newspapers became the main tools for information dissemination, though social interaction was limited by geography and communication speed.

At the end of the 19th and beginning of the 20th centuries, the advent of the telegraph shortened information transmission time, and the proliferation of telephones changed long-distance communication, enabling people to exchange information more swiftly. The emergence of radio and television media in the 20th century altered mass communication, allowing information to spread more widely and shaping cultural, political, and social views.

From the 1990s to the early 2000s, the advent of the Internet-enabled broader and more immediate information dissemination. The Web 1.0 era was primarily composed of static web pages, with content mostly being one-way transmissions from officials to users, offering little opportunity for user interaction or content creation.

From the mid-2000s onwards, the rise of Web 2.0 introduced social media platforms that emphasized interaction and user participation. Facebook, a pioneer of Web 2.0 social interaction, provided functionalities for sharing information, photos, videos, and status updates, allowing users to build social networks. Subsequently, platforms like Twitter, YouTube, LinkedIn, and in China, Weibo, WeChat, Douyin, and Xiaohongshu emerged, offering various user-generated content and social features, becoming primary tools for everyday communication, sharing, and interaction.

Each platform has its unique features and functions. For example, Twitter and Weibo are crucial platforms for information dissemination and social interaction due to their unique real-time messaging. YouTube and Douyin, as video sharing platforms, have changed how people watch and share videos, becoming popular platforms for content creation and sharing. LinkedIn focuses on professional networking, offering a platform for users to build professional relationships, share work experiences, and expand networks. Instagram, with its powerful image-sharing features, attracts numerous users, becoming a primary platform for photo and video sharing.

In the Web 2.0 era, emphasizing user participation, platforms transitioned from static pages to dynamic social hubs, enabling content creation and sharing. This evolution, fueled by mobile Internet and smartphones, allowed users to engage with social media ubiquitously, catalyzing both personal interaction and commercial utilization. Companies leveraged these platforms for marketing, propelling the commercial value of social projects.

Yet, beneath Web 2.0's thriving interactivity, underlying issues loomed, centered around data ownership and centralization. User data, the cornerstone of Web 2.0's social platforms, often didn't belong to the users but to the platforms, raising concerns over privacy and data misuse. This led to a scenario where platforms could commodify and exploit user data without equitable compensation, creating a lopsided value exchange.

Data silos emerged, with users' information confined to individual platforms, obstructing the seamless transfer of profiles and social connections across different networks. Content creators, the value drivers of these platforms, faced challenges in asserting control and reaping benefits from their contributions. The platforms' terms often granted them unchecked rights to user-generated content, compromising creators' intellectual property rights.

Centralization further exacerbated issues of censorship and freedom of expression. Users' content, subject to the platforms' control, could be arbitrarily moderated or removed, underscoring vulnerabilities in preserving users' rights to free speech. Attempts at decentralization, like Mastodon, though well-intentioned, couldn't fully escape the grasp of centralization, with users still potentially under the sway of server providers.

Web 3.0 social networking emerges as a response, leveraging blockchain and decentralized frameworks to envision a social space where users have greater control and security. This new paradigm aims to rectify Web 2.0's pitfalls, offering a platform where user data, content, and interactions are safeguarded by blockchain technology, promising a more liberated and secure digital social environment.

3.1.2 Web 3.0 Social Networking Value Proposition

In comparison with Web 2.0 social platforms, Web 3.0 social networking offers significant advantages, particularly in terms of value and power redistribution.

First, Web 3.0 social networking facilitates the rediscovery and more equitable distribution of values that were overlooked or captured by platforms in Web 2.0. This includes user sovereignty, where Web 3.0 social media returns ownership back to individual users. Utilizing blockchain data and decentralized nodes ensures users have sovereignty over their data, including consumption habits, preferences, privacy, digital assets, and identity. This design empowers users to manage and control their information autonomously, freeing them from centralized platform constraints, thus enhancing individuals' power in digital social spaces. Additionally, it reshapes the creator economy. In this new social system, content creators become the "true controllers." For instance, creators can monetize by acquiring platform tokens based on quantifiable metrics like clicks and shares. Web 3.0 also offers creators diverse revenue channels. By minting content NFTs, creators not only protect their copyrights but also profit from secondary market sales, providing a more sustainable income source.

Second, compared to Web 2.0, Web 3.0 social platforms have significantly revamped governance mechanisms, partially decentralizing governance to the community. This shift transfers content moderation and ownership decision-making from centralized platforms to community members, granting them greater participation and decision-making power.

Third, the traditional Web 2.0 social environment creates a pain point in digital identity management, with users' digital identities being non-interoperable across platforms. Web 3.0 addresses this by introducing a mechanism for decentralized identity connectivity, aiming to create a universal digital identity that enables users to navigate various social scenarios on more open and composable protocols.

Last, Web 3.0 social innovation allows users' actions or outcomes to be tokenized, creating new asset forms and broadening the ways these assets can be traded and rights assigned. This introduces novel collaboration methods and value distribution mechanisms for social platform users, creating richer and more diverse possibilities for social engagement.

In summary, Web 3.0 social networking, through its value and power redistribution, enhanced governance, universal digital identity, and tokenization of social interactions, presents a more equitable, decentralized, and innovative digital social landscape compared to the constraints of Web 2.0 social platforms.

3.1.3 Attempts at Web 3.0 Social Networking

In the evolving landscape of Web 3.0 social networking, the emphasis on decentralization, user empowerment, and resistance to censorship stands out, delineating a new frontier for innovation and break-throughs in digital interaction. This new era in social networking is stratified across four integral layers: application, protocol, blockchain, and storage, each playing a pivotal role in the ecosystem's functionality and user experience.

At the apex, the application layer interfaces directly with users, offering a spectrum of social utilities and scenarios, from social media platforms to gaming and community engagement spaces. This layer is where users first encounter the Web 3.0 social networking experience, serving as the gateway to a broader realm of decentralized interaction.

Beneath this, the protocol layer serves as the backbone for development, offering standardized components and foundational protocols that catalyze product creation. This layer democratizes development, enabling a diverse array of applications to emerge and fostering a rich ecosystem of social networking tools that cater to various user needs.

The blockchain layer underpins the ecosystem, ensuring data exchanges are decentralized, secure, and transparent. It's here that social-specific blockchains provide tailored solutions to meet the unique demands of social applications, ensuring scalability, speed, and security.

At the base, the storage layer ensures the integrity and accessibility of social data, employing decentralized storage solutions to safeguard user-generated content and interaction histories, thereby enhancing user trust and control over their data.

Together, these layers form a synergistic structure that propels Web 3.0 social networking forward, enabling a versatile array of applications that respond to diverse user needs and scenarios. As this sector continues to mature, various Web 3.0 social projects are emerging, each exploring unique approaches to value reciprocation, censorship resistance, and the creation of novel social environments, marking a dynamic period of exploration and growth in the digital social domain.

• **DATA-VALUE-BASED WEB 3.0 SOCIAL NETWORKING**

In the arena of value-centric Web 3.0 social networking, the paradigm shifts from treating user data as an asset owned by platforms to recognizing it as the rightful property of the users themselves. Traditionally, social platforms utilized user data for targeted advertising and personalized marketing, but unfortunately, the value generated from this data seldom circled back to benefit the users. In essence, users' data contributions were exploited freely by platforms without due compensation, leading to a scenario where the value of user data was "freely harvested."

In this model, whether it's the value of content created by users or the personal data they provide, the majority of the generated profits are monopolized by the platforms, leaving users and creators with minimal gains from the value exchange. However, new Web 3.0 social products are seeking to overturn this model by employing mechanisms like token incentives and NFTization of data. Notable examples of Web 3.0 social projects include Lens Protocol, Friend.tech, and Bodhi.

Lens Protocol, a decentralized social graph protocol, was founded by the team behind the DeFi lending project Aave on February 8, 2022, and operates on the Polygon blockchain. Its distinguishing feature is that all user-owned social graph data—including personal profiles, content sharing and posting, comments, and social relationships—are stored as NFTs.

The Lens Protocol is characterized by three primary features:

(1) Tradable data value. Traditional social media doesn't adequately reward users or creators for their valuable contributions. Lens Protocol addresses this by NFTizing user data, allowing for the free market trading of accounts as NFTs. While most people are likely to maintain strong ties to their social accounts, reducing the likelihood of trading, the potential market value

for user account trades introduces an interesting question.

(2) Protocol layer integration. Lens provides modular components for social dApp developers, enabling the creation of innovative social products. User data, now NFTized, is controlled via DID, allowing for data synchronization across different applications and facilitating data portability.

(3) High decentralization. Content, social interactions, and identities in Lens Protocol are all recorded on the blockchain. Various products, like Lenster and Phaver, have been developed on Lens, with Lenster functioning similarly to Twitter, providing a decentralized social media experience.

Friend.tech focuses on tokenizing individual influence, turning it into an economic model for fans and KOLs (key opinion leaders). Users can buy a KOL's "key" to join private chats and gain from the appreciation of the key's value as the KOL's influence grows. KOLs, in turn, benefit financially from their expanding influence and the associated transaction fees on their tokens.

Bodhi emphasizes content assetization, similar to Friend.tech's reputation assetization but focuses on individual content items. This specificity broadens the scope of transactions, making them more focused. Content on Bodhi is stored on Arweave, ensuring decentralized storage.

In the realm of reciprocating data value back to users, whether it's the protocol layer's Lens Protocol or application-oriented platforms like Friend.tech and Bodhi, various approaches are being explored to address this need.

The Lens Protocol employs a method of tokenizing users' social graph data, allowing personal profiles and content data to be controlled as NFTs under Decentralized Identifiers (DID) and traded freely on the market, creating transaction opportunities for high-value accounts. Additionally, Lens's modular components offer social dApp developers data liquidity, enabling user data synchronization and circulation across different applications. On the other hand, Friend.tech tokenizes the reputation of KOLs, allowing fans to buy a "key" to join private groups and benefit from the KOL's influence and monetary incentives. These projects employ value monetization mechanisms, enabling users and creators to share the value of their data and content more equitably. Such innovative social products return the value of user data to the users themselves, facilitating the liquidity and tradability of data value through various mechanisms.

- **ANTI-CENSORSHIP WEB 3.0 SOCIAL NETWORKING**
In addition to incentivizing data value, combating censorship is a pivotal focus in current Web 3.0 initiatives. Traditional Web 2.0 social platforms are often plagued by centralized management, which can impose significant constraints on content censorship and freedom of speech. In contrast, Web 3.0 social networking champions decentralization, reducing dependency on any central platform and diminishing the risks of censorship and account suspensions, thus promoting a more open environment for free expression. Two notable projects in this arena are Farcaster and Nostr.

Farcaster, a decentralized social protocol, empowers developers to create user-centric social applications. Founded by Dan and Varun, former senior executives at Coinbase, Farcaster has garnered strong backing from notable figures like Vitalik Buterin. Its key features include a decentralized identity and an enhanced user experience, achieved through a blend of on-chain and off-chain elements. It secures users' identity information on the blockchain, facilitating decentralized identities. Analogous to Lens, Farcaster ties data to user identities, enabling seamless transitions between applications within its ecosystem at low migration costs. In addition to identity data, Farcaster offloads high-frequency information, such as user posts and interactions, to Farcaster Hub, an off-chain repository, ensuring swift data transmission and a superior user experience.

Nostr, an open-source, decentralized social protocol developed by an enigmatic team with a focus on anti-censorship, was conceptualized by Fiatjaf, a developer known for his work on Bitcoin and the Lightning Network. Its distinctive architecture comprises clients and "relays." Anyone can host a relay, maintaining independence and interacting solely with users. Users possess public and private keys, akin to mailbox addresses and keys, facilitating secure message exchanges, with unique private key signatures authenticating the sender's identity. A recipient's private key, or "mailbox key," guarantees message receipt.

Damus, built atop the Nostr protocol, is akin to X yet decentralized. Each Damus participant functions as a client within a network of numerous relays. The open nature of relay operation precludes incidents akin to censorship seen on X. Users are free to choose any relay, including their own, for publishing content, maximizing anti-censorship capabilities.

Despite the ascendance of platforms like Mastodon, emphasizing anti-censorship, centralized management on Web 2.0 platforms often curtails content and speech. As blockchain technology advances, a growing number of Web 3.0 projects aim to forge censorship-resistant counterparts to X, Facebook, and other social platforms and protocols.

Farcaster and Nostr are laudable endeavors in this context. While neither has yet cultivated continuously active applications and Farcaster's user base is relatively modest compared to Web 2.0 entities, its substantial post and interaction metrics already indicate user engagement. These initiatives herald new prospects for anti-censorship in Web 3.0 social networking, offering valuable insights and fostering optimism for the emergence of future pivotal applications.

- **WEB 3.0'S NATIVE SOCIAL SCENARIOS**

In the realm of Web 3.0, blockchain technology not only addresses issues of user data value reciprocity and anti-censorship but also introduces native social functionalities. Various projects are delving into specialized scenarios to fulfill these inherent social needs, with DeBox being a prime example.

DeBox tackles the "hold-to-chat" challenge prevalent in traditional group chats, whether they involve tokens or NFTs. Typically, it's difficult to prevent outsiders from infiltrating these chats, which can lead to risks like scams and market manipulation. DeBox's group chat feature mandates that members must hold specific NFTs or a certain amount of tokens to join the community, creating a consensus-driven group environment.

In its initial phase, DeBox leveraged several NFT collections to kickstart its platform, successfully drawing a substantial user base. By forming communities grounded on shared holdings, DeBox unites members with aligned interests and perspectives. This model promotes organic community governance and minimizes information noise. With content storage and logic maintained off-chain, DeBox delivers a user experience akin to that of Web 2.0 social platforms, seamlessly integrating advanced Web 3.0 features while maintaining user familiarity and ease of use.

3.1.4 Navigating the Challenges of Web 3.0 Social Networking

The journey of Web 3.0 social networking toward mainstream acceptance is still in progress, facing several substantial hurdles, with user experience at the forefront of these challenges. Web 3.0 platforms, which typically require wallet logins, can seem foreign to users accustomed to the traditional sign-up and login processes of Web 2.0. While this wallet-based authentication aligns with the decentralization ethos of Web 3.0, empowering users over their identities and assets, it demands a significant shift in user behavior, adapting to new mechanisms of identity verification and digital asset management. This transition not only restricts general access to Web 3.0 social offerings but also challenges their development and broader acceptance. Moreover, the complexities of blockchain and cryptocurrency concepts necessitate user education, potentially imposing an additional learning burden.

The inherent trade-off between decentralization and efficiency presents another dilemma. Total on-chain processing can burden user interactions, prompting projects to explore various strategies. Some store all content, connections, and identities on-chain, while others opt for a hybrid approach, balancing user experience with on-chain integration. Full on-chain storage may introduce issues related to costs and transaction speeds, while partial storage might lead users to question the authenticity of the decentralization claim. Resolving what to store on-chain to optimize both user experience and practicality is an ongoing process for Web 3.0 initiatives.

Moreover, the entrenched positions of platforms like Facebook and Twitter, with their strong network effects and user loyalty, present high switching costs for users considering transitioning to Web 3.0 platforms. Users must evaluate the benefits of new experiences against the costs of leaving an established network, where they've invested significant time and effort.

If Web 3.0 social platforms offer little beyond a decentralized version of Web 2.0 experiences, they may struggle to attract users, especially when the typical user may not fully grasp the nuances of decentralized storage but is acutely aware of their user experience and the direct costs of transitioning.

To surmount these hurdles, Web 3.0 social networking must deliver innovative user experiences. Intuitive interfaces, flexible social connection methods, and creative content presentation underpinned by blockchain and smart contracts can foster a transparent, equitable, and engaging environment. These innovations are crucial for Web 3.0 social networking to provide a compelling alternative to Web 2.0, fostering wider adoption and engagement.

In essence, the evolution of social interaction continues, with Web 3.0 introducing a new chapter emphasizing anti-censorship and user data empowerment. While Web 3.0 has yet to match Web 2.0 in scale, the underlying demand for these features is accumulating, setting the stage for future breakthroughs in how we connect and interact online.

3.2 Web 3.0 in Gaming

Historical experiences show that gaming is one of the most potent sectors in driving breakthroughs in Internet evolution, achieving significant success from Web 1.0 to 2.0. In the exploration of widespread applications for Web 3.0, gaming is considered a promising field with the potential to create breakout applications. This emerging domain offers players genuine ownership and economic incentives, introducing new possibilities to the gaming industry.

3.2.1 Understanding Web 3.0 Gaming
Web 3.0 gaming refers to game projects that enhance user experiences and alter traditional gaming paradigms using blockchain technology,

cryptocurrencies, and NFTs. The primary goal of Web 3.0 games is to empower players with more control and ownership through decentralization, digital ownership, and economic incentives, creating more authentic, transparent, and engaging experiences.

A game must be enjoyable at its core, offering a sense of thrill rooted in fundamental emotional factors inherent in our genetic makeup. Additionally, games should provide novelty, spark curiosity and a desire for challenge, and reward players with unpredictable rewards and a sense of achievement.

Web 2.0 games focus on sensory depth, pure playability, and thrill, often set in open worlds and virtual environments. They also emphasize sensory breadth, highlighting social incentives and ranking systems, with game data assets leading the way in earning rewards and social recognition.

Theoretically, Web 3.0 games are as engaging as MMORPGs, puzzle games, and strategy games from the Web 2.0 era. However, unlike Web 2.0, where centralized developers control games, players in Web 3.0 games have true ownership of in-game assets. Blockchain technology and smart contracts in Web 3.0 provide a real opportunity for players to own digital assets both in and out of games.

Blockchain's decentralization accurately records the ownership of virtual items on an immutable ledger, while smart contracts ensure the authenticity and tradability of these digital assets. Combined with NFT technology, Web 3.0 grants complete ownership of virtual assets to users. Each NFT is unique, with its own identity and value, allowing free trade and transfer of digital assets in and out of the game.

Web 3.0 gaming's core innovation is the absolute control users have over virtual assets, changing ownership dynamics both in and out of games and granting players more autonomy. In Web 2.0, players' time and money spent on games couldn't be converted into real-world value. In contrast,

Web 3.0 allows players to freely transfer their NFTs and digital assets to other games or platforms, or trade them in digital markets, creating a new gaming experience where virtual efforts are reflected in reality.

Moreover, Web 3.0 gaming breaks the monopoly that traditional game companies have over game rules. Decentralized governance allows players to participate in decision-making, making games more democratic and attracting active player involvement in their development. This community governance not only strengthens the game community's cohesion but also provides game companies with diverse and objective feedback, improving game quality and playability.

In essence, Web 3.0 hasn't changed the quality of games but has opened doors to new financial systems within gaming. This transformation alters the player-game relationship and introduces new business models and possibilities to the gaming industry.

3.2.2 The Transformation in the Gaming Industry

The primary distinction between Web 3.0 and Web 2.0 games is that Web 3.0 games can monetize in-game assets through NFTs, bringing financial benefits to players.

First, NFTs give tangible value to game assets through asset confirmation rights. This right mechanism not only ensures players' control but also enhances their creative rights. Players can encapsulate the time and skills accumulated in the game into NFTs, granting them creation, transfer, and profit rights in the game. This confirmation of rights transforms players' efforts and investments into actual digital assets, expanding their creative and profit opportunities.

Second, NFT assets have intrinsic utility value in-game, allowing players to engage in activities like gold farming, voting, and minting new NFTs. Smart contracts enhance the trust players place in the game due to their anti-cheating features. Some games with governance voting systems even allow players to decide the game's direction and ensure execution based on their token holdings. This governance mechanism democratizes and opens up the game, encouraging player participation in decision-making and fostering community development.

Last, NFT assets have external market value, not limited to the game's internal environment. Players can freely trade and transfer their NFT assets and game tokens on the blockchain, enjoying liquidity premiums and social value. Especially rare NFT assets become a form of wealth and skill, thus attracting attention and social recognition. Additionally, the transparency of blockchain data allows developers to target accounts holding rare assets precisely, enhancing the marketing value of NFT assets.

Several games have emerged in the Web 3.0 gaming space, such as *AssetClub*, *League of Thrones*, and *Townstory Galaxy*, each offering unique features and contributing to the evolving landscape of Web 3.0 gaming.

Moreover, the "play-to-earn" game model is a groundbreaking concept in Web 3.0 gaming, with *Axie* Infinity being a notable pioneer. Unlike traditional free-to-play models or staking mechanisms in blockchain projects, play-to-earn allows players to earn game tokens through active participation, akin to a proof of work (PoW) reward system.

Axie Infinity's dual-token system, incorporating AXS and SLP tokens, establishes its token economy, where players can earn rewards through various in-game activities. This model has even fostered new ecosystems like blockchain gaming guilds, offering asset rental services and enabling cost-free player participation in games.

In conclusion, Web 3.0 games stand out not just for their graphics, sound effects, or smooth mechanics but for their unique governance models and features like immutability, composability, and openness, offering players an unparalleled gaming experience. Web 3.0 games fully embrace the decentralized, transparent, and open ethos of Web 3.0, encouraging active participation from all stakeholders. Additionally, NFT technology ensures the utmost protection of players' in-game creations and achievements, potentially fostering a new commercial ecosystem centered around gaming.

3.3 Web 3.0 in Finance

Web 3.0 finance is emerging swiftly, distinguishing itself from Web 2.0 finance, especially in the context of ownership and earnings. In the conventional Web 2.0 financial markets, profits were dominated by investors and Wall Street bankers, the titans of traditional markets, where ordinary individuals seldom felt empowered. In contrast, Web 3.0 has fostered a unique financial ecosystem where money and earnings circulate among the populace, giving rise to decentralized exchanges (Dex) and DeFi. The future of Web 3.0 finance is set to redefine the financial services landscape, offering vast growth opportunities for the financial market.

3.3.1 A Battle for Information

Finance fundamentally involves managing money, encompassing activities like savings, loans, investments, budgeting, and forecasting. It's viewed as a social tool for managing resources, risks, and returns across time and space, with financial services now accounting for about 20% of the global GDP.

In finance, information is pivotal. Timely and accurate information underpins financial decisions. In markets like stocks, bonds, and forex, the speed and quality of information acquisition directly impact the success of transactions. Traditionally, Wall Street giants operated on informational and resource advantages, establishing extensive information networks to gain market insights. This provided them with a competitive edge, enabling them to make informed investment decisions promptly.

Informational advantages also extend to deep insights into customer needs and market trends. Through comprehensive data analysis and market research, financial institutions can tailor their products and services to meet market demands, enhancing customer relationships.

Moreover, effective risk management is another facet of informational advantage. The financial market is fraught with uncertainties and volatility. Precise and timely risk assessments are crucial for financial institutions' sustainability and growth.

Entering the Internet era, this informational advantage has been gradually eroded. The advent of electronic quotes and automated matching trades has made financial asset pricing more transparent. While major transactions or complex structured deals still require professional institutions, they constitute a small fraction of all financial trades.

The speed at which financial news, corporate announcements, and regulatory information spread has dramatically increased. Investors no longer need analysts to relay or interpret this information. The "voice" in capital markets has been decentralized to numerous media and individuals. Enhanced transparency has also made investors more price-sensitive, enabling easy comparisons across different service providers.

As information advantage wanes, traditional investment banks and capital market businesses face dwindling profits, pushing them toward proprietary trading and reliance on complex, non-standardized financial derivatives. These products may command higher fees but carry immense risks, as evidenced by the downfall of major institutions during the subprime mortgage crisis.

In response, global regulators have tightened oversight on large financial institutions, limiting proprietary trading to maintain higher capital ratios. Surviving Wall Street giants have shifted focus to more stable businesses like asset management, private wealth management, and consumer finance.

Furthermore, traditional financial institutions show signs of exhaustion in financial services, opening opportunities for Web 2.0 fintech (financial technology) innovations. Since 2014, fintech, including mobile payments, microloans, and cryptocurrencies, has captured global capital market attention. Apple, with its extensive fintech initiatives, exemplifies this trend. Apple Pay, introduced in 2014, Apple Card, in partnership with Goldman Sachs in 2019, and Apple Pay Later in 2023, showcase Apple's strategic foray into finance, leveraging data as a key asset.

While fintech in Web 2.0 has advanced inclusive finance to some extent, it has also birthed new challenges, signaling the need for the transformative potential of Web 3.0 in the financial sector:

(1) Centralization and monopoly issues in finance. Centralized financial platforms and corporations typically monopolize the market, controlling users' financial data and transaction information. This centralized financial model leads to various issues, including information leakage, data misuse, and monopolistic pricing. Centralized platforms store vast amounts of sensitive user information, making them prime targets for cyberattacks, potentially leading to identity theft

and fraud. Moreover, these platforms might use or sell user data for commercial purposes, raising privacy concerns and diminishing trust in financial platforms.

(2) Opacity in transactions and settlements. In Web 2.0 finance, transaction and settlement processes often lack transparency, creating several issues for users. In traditional centralized financial systems, it's challenging for users to track the flow of funds clearly. Centralized institutions manage users' funds, and users can't readily access or verify transaction details, leading to information asymmetry. Additionally, centralized platforms might include opaque fees during transactions and settlements, increasing users' transaction costs and reducing financial service transparency.

Web 3.0 technology offers new possibilities to address these issues. By leveraging blockchain technology and smart contracts, Web 3.0 finance achieves decentralized transactions and settlements, greatly enhancing transparency. Blockchain's distributed ledger ensures accurate recording of each transaction, allowing users to view and verify transaction details in real-time. Smart contracts automate transactions and settlements, reducing uncertainty and enhancing reliability.

Moreover, Web 3.0's decentralized nature makes transactions and settlements more flexible and open. Users can conduct financial activities globally without geographical or regulatory restrictions, offering more convenient and efficient financial services worldwide.

Web 3.0 also significantly impacts the financial industry by further eliminating information asymmetry and enhancing risk management efficiency. Finance inherently deals with risk: every financial asset and customer entails unique risks, and the market is influenced by systemic and numerous non-systemic risks. In an era of information asymmetry, financial institutions had to control risks through collateral and guarantees, focusing on having a backup plan rather than ensuring no issues arise.

For instance, many truck drivers have obtained loans by "tokenizing" their truck assets, making it easier to sell the trucks. SME owners can reduce financing costs and enhance production safety by tokenizing their equipment. These transactions don't necessarily need to occur on public chains but can take place on trusted private chains, like those operated by financial institutions or professional intermediaries. This not only lowers the difficulty for SMEs and individuals to access financial services but also reduces the overall risk in the financial system.

3.3.2 Applications of Web 3.0 Finance

Currently, Web 3.0 finance has given rise to Dex and DeFi, which are altering the rules of the financial market and reshaping the financial landscape.

- **DEXS**

DeFi complements the evolution of DEXs by extending blockchain's scope beyond simple asset exchange. DeFi represents a broad category of financial applications in cryptocurrency or blockchain geared toward disrupting financial intermediaries. It leverages blockchain technology to eliminate intermediaries in financial transactions, enabling everything from lending and borrowing platforms to stablecoins and tokenized BTC.

DeFi platforms operate on the principle that cryptocurrency holders should have access to all financial services without needing a bank or other traditional financial institution. This autonomy is made possible through the use of smart contracts, which automatically execute the terms of an agreement based on coded conditions. This innovation not only increases the speed and reduces the cost of financial transactions but also introduces a level of transparency and security previously unattainable in traditional finance.

Moreover, DeFi has democratized access to financial services. Users anywhere in the world with an Internet connection can lend out their assets and earn interest or take out a loan without going through a credit check, provided they have sufficient cryptocurrency to use as collateral. This accessibility is reshaping who can participate in financial markets and, on what terms, potentially altering the global financial landscape in profound ways.

However, the nascent DeFi sector is not without its risks, including those associated with early-stage technology, regulatory uncertainty, and the volatility of cryptocurrency markets. The sector's reliance on smart contracts, which are only as reliable as the code they're written with, adds another layer of risk. Despite these challenges, the promise of DeFi—a more accessible, efficient, and transparent financial system—continues to attract significant interest from both users and investors, signaling a robust area of growth within the broader Web 3.0 framework.

- **DEFI APPLICATIONS**

DeFi represents a transformative movement within the financial sector, leveraging blockchain and oracle technologies to redefine the landscape of traditional financial services. This paradigm shift aims to dismantle the constraints of centralized financial systems, ushering in a more open, transparent, and decentralized ecosystem.

At its core, DeFi applications harness the power of blockchain technology and smart contracts to innovate and diversify financial products, encompassing lending, trading, and the issuance of stablecoins, among others. These smart contracts automate and streamline financial protocols, eliminating the need for intermediaries. This not only enhances the efficiency of transactions but also significantly reduces associated costs, providing users with a direct and more agile experience of financial activities on the blockchain.

Furthermore, DeFi leverages oracle technology to bridge the gap between blockchains and external data sources. Oracles facilitate the integration of real-world data into blockchain ecosystems, enabling smart contracts to execute decisions based on this external information. This integration expands the utility of DeFi applications, allowing them to explore new domains such as insurance and prediction markets, thus broadening the scope of financial services available within the DeFi ecosystem.

The overarching aim of Web 3.0 finance is to forge an open, robust, and transparent financial system that significantly reduces dependence on centralized authorities. This ambition aligns with the broader objectives of Web 3.0, which advocate for decentralization and user empowerment. Consequently, the adoption and continual innovation of blockchain and cryptographic technologies are pivotal in shaping a new era of finance— one that is more inclusive, efficient, and attuned to the needs of a digitally evolving world.

3.4 Web 3.0 in Healthcare

The advent of Web 3.0 is set to revolutionize the healthcare industry, offering innovative solutions to manage the burgeoning volume of medical data. In recent years, the healthcare sector has seen a surge in data generation, sourced from an array of systems, devices, and sensors. This data encompasses a wide spectrum of medical information, including patient symptoms, observational outcomes, diagnoses, treatments, and medication details, typically stored in electronic health records (EHRs), electronic medical records (EMRs), and various practice management systems. The depth and breadth of this data enable advanced systems to draw intricate connections between disparate symptoms, paving the way for more accurate diagnoses and tailored treatment plans.

Nonetheless, the healthcare sector faces a significant challenge: the data stored in EHRs, EMRs, and related systems are often confined within isolated information silos. This compartmentalization hinders the seamless exchange and integration of vital medical information, limiting the potential for comprehensive and coordinated patient care. Web 3.0 heralds a transformative era for healthcare, promising to dismantle these silos and foster a more interconnected and accessible data environment.

3.4.1 Dismantling Centralized Control in Healthcare

In the realm of healthcare, traditional models have predominantly embraced centralized management structures, where a handful of authoritative entities hold sway over the vast majority of medical data, resources, and decision-making processes. This centralization sees patients' medical records, diagnostic information, treatment histories, and other sensitive data predominantly under the stewardship of select healthcare facilities, medical professionals, and insurance entities. While this model has long been the norm, it introduces several critical issues and challenges that impede the industry's progress and efficiency.

One primary concern with this centralized approach is the lack of transparency and security surrounding medical data. Typically, patients' health information is ensconced within the databases of healthcare providers and centralized information systems, creating substantial vulnerabilities. Such a setup poses heightened risks of data breaches and misuse, where patients often remain in the dark about the whereabouts and utilization of their personal health information, compromising their privacy and data security.

Moreover, the centralized healthcare model exacerbates the power imbalance between healthcare providers and patients. With medical professionals and institutions holding the reins over patients' data, an information asymmetry emerges, skewing the doctor-patient relationship. This dynamic often results in patients having minimal say in their healthcare decisions, reducing their ability to actively engage in their medical care and ensuring their needs and perspectives are adequately considered.

Additionally, centralized management hampers innovation within the healthcare sector. Medical advancements often hinge on the availability and accessibility of extensive datasets. However, in a centralized system, data sharing across different entities is fraught with challenges, limiting the scope and depth of potential research and innovation, which is crucial for developing new therapies, advancing drug research, and enhancing disease prevention strategies.

The pharmaceutical supply chain, too, suffers under centralized management, with opacity at each juncture from production to distribution, complicating the traceability of medications and elevating the risks associated with counterfeit or substandard drugs.

Operational inefficiencies and heightened costs also plague the centralized healthcare model. The demands of sustaining a large centralized system—spanning hardware maintenance, software updates, and cybersecurity measures—not only incur significant expenses but also introduce operational complexities. Additionally, the lack of uniform technical standards and data interoperability among healthcare entities further impedes efficient information exchange, affecting the timeliness and accuracy of healthcare delivery.

In response to these myriad issues, a shift toward decentralization is emerging, spearheaded by the principles of Web 3.0. This new paradigm promises to democratize healthcare, offering a framework where data is more transparent, secure, and user-controlled, fostering a more equitable and efficient healthcare ecosystem. Through decentralization, Web 3.0 healthcare envisages a future where patient empowerment and data sovereignty are paramount, catalyzing a more innovative, responsive, and patient-centric healthcare landscape.

3.4.2 The Transformative Impact of Web 3.0 on Healthcare

Web 3.0 heralds a paradigm shift in healthcare, transcending mere technological advancement to redefine data security, transparency, and the dynamics between healthcare providers and patients, unlocking new possibilities across the spectrum.

First, Web 3.0 technologies foster a more secure and transparent framework for medical data management, benefiting both patients and healthcare providers through decentralization. This approach distributes medical data across a network rather than centralizing it, with patients having unique identifiers and healthcare entities accessing specific data only with patient consent. This model minimizes the risks of data breaches and misuse, thereby protecting patient privacy. Smart contracts can set and enforce data access rules, granting patients control over their data and bolstering trust in privacy management.

The transparency inherent in Web 3.0 enhances medical data traceability. Each data interaction, whether access, modification, or sharing, is immutable on the blockchain, offering a clear data lineage that builds trust in the healthcare system. This level of transparency can also cut healthcare costs by optimizing the use of medical reports and avoiding redundant tests.

Moreover, Web 3.0 reshapes healthcare insurance and the doctor-patient relationship. Patients can use smart contracts to manage data sharing, playing a proactive role in their care, reducing information asymmetry, and fostering trust. Such patient involvement tailors treatment plans more closely to individual needs. Decentralized governance allows patient feedback on healthcare services, potentially establishing a transparent service rating system through smart contracts, which could motivate providers to enhance service quality.

Beyond patient data decentralization, Web 3.0 introduces innovative solutions for global health data sharing. By harnessing smart contracts and encryption technology, the medical field anticipates the construction of a secure, controllable global health data sharing network. Here, smart contracts play a pivotal role in defining data access permissions, usage conditions, and durations, ensuring that only authorized entities can access specific health data. This approach effectively addresses privacy and security concerns prevalent in traditional health data sharing, laying a more reliable foundation for global medical research. Encryption technology ensures the privacy of health data; advanced encryption algorithms protect data during transmission and storage, mitigating the risks of unauthorized access or alteration. This encryption mechanism boosts the trustworthiness of global health data sharing, encouraging more active participation.

A global health data sharing network based on Web 3.0 allows health institutions, research entities, and international organizations to share and access health data more efficiently. This facilitates a better understanding of disease transmission patterns, enhancing prediction and prevention strategies. Moreover, the integration of global health data supports more extensive and in-depth transnational disease research, fostering international medical research collaboration.

Web 3.0's application in healthcare extends to pharmaceutical research and distribution. In drug development, blockchain's transparency injects higher credibility into the entire R&D process. Traditionally stored research data, often held by pharmaceutical companies or research institutions, faced questions of information asymmetry and credibility. Blockchain technology allows research data to be transparently recorded, ensuring data authenticity and immutability, enhancing research data credibility, and providing a more transparent and secure foundation for the pharmaceutical R&D ecosystem.

Smart contracts optimize the efficiency and safety of drug distribution. They can automate and make the pharmaceutical supply chain transparent, allowing real-time sharing of production, inventory, and distribution information among healthcare institutions, pharmaceutical companies, and distributors. This decentralized distribution model promises to improve the timeliness and accessibility of medications, ensuring patients receive effective treatment when needed.

Web 3.0's application in healthcare is not just a technological improvement but a complete revolution of the healthcare system, aiming to make medical services safer, more transparent, and equitable, driving the industry toward more advanced and humane development. This has profound significance and value for establishing an open, resilient, and transparent healthcare system for all.

PART TWO

Web 3.0 in the Age of Web 3.0

In the previous discourse, we engaged in a reflection on Web 3.0, largely anchored in the present-day technological landscape. This reflection, predominantly rooted in the technologies and societal understandings of the Web 2.0 era, provided a glimpse into what we might perceive as Web 3.0 today. However, it's crucial to acknowledge that this portrayal is merely a transitional phase, not the full embodiment of Web 3.0's potential. Hence, the earlier discussions were framed within the context of Web 3.0 as seen through the lens of the Web 2.0 era.

Looking forward, the genuine essence of Web 3.0, which we anticipate in the future, will likely diverge significantly from our current observations. It is poised to emerge as a natural evolution, propelled by a convergence of advanced technologies, heralding a new chapter in Internet history. Whether this future iteration will retain the moniker "Web 3.0" or adopt a new designation remains to be seen. For now, our discourse adheres to the prevailing consensus on what constitutes Web 3.0.

In the ensuing sections, I aim to venture beyond the current paradigm, offering a forward-looking analysis of the revolutionary technologies that will shape the next generation of the Internet, delving into Web 3.0 from the vantage point of the Web 3.0 era itself.

To embark on this exploration, we must first clarify our understanding of Web 3.0. Here, I propose defining Web 3.0 as an era of "digital sovereignty." This forthcoming era symbolizes a significant transformation and reconfiguration of civilization, marking a transition where individuals in the digital domain assert sovereignty over their digital identities and actions. Web 3.0 heralds a shift from the traditional civil rights of the non-digital era to a new paradigm where digital sovereignty reigns supreme.

With this conceptual framework as our guide, we will delve into the multifaceted nature of Web 3.0 in the era of digital sovereignty, unraveling its implications, challenges, and opportunities in the forthcoming discussions.

—CHAPTER 4—

The Web 2.0 and the Web 3.0

4.1 Web 3.0 Trapped in Web 2.0

Currently, Web 3.0 is increasingly becoming a topic of conversation, with the concepts and theories surrounding it rapidly gaining traction. Rather than a mere proliferation of ideas, it's more accurate to describe this phase as exploratory. Similar to the early discussions about the metaverse, the current discourse may not precisely capture the future, as many of the underlying technologies are still evolving and maturing. The most accurate foresight into Web 3.0 can be achieved by viewing it through the lens of advanced technological developments.

In simple terms, Web 3.0 represents the next era of the Internet. It envisions an Internet that is accessible to all, founded on open protocols and transparent blockchain networks, and fosters a society built on communication technologies. Web 3.0 is, in essence, a societal aspiration toward freedom and democracy, explored through technological advancements. It is grounded on open-source protocols and commercial interfaces, aiming to redesign existing Internet services and products to benefit the public, offering easy access and a host of other features.

Contrasting sharply with the centralized nature of Web 2.0, Web 3.0 champions decentralization. At this stage, decentralization is considered a fundamental characteristic of Web 3.0. However, it's also the stage's most significant challenge—the current understanding of Web 3.0 is largely a response to the issues presented by Web 2.0, a hopeful vision rather than a realized one. Can decentralization truly be achieved? What is the likelihood that Web 3.0 will break the monopolistic trends of Web 2.0? These are the pressing questions as we delve deeper into the evolving landscape of Web 3.0.

4.1.1 The Illusion of Web 3.0

During the latter half of 2021, as discussions around Web 3.0 gained momentum, various entities—individuals, businesses, and organizations—hurriedly joined the bandwagon, making Web 3.0 a trending topic. The swift market embrace of Web 3.0 also attracted significant investment. But what spurred the emergence of the Web 3.0 concept? Fundamentally, from the Web's inception to its evolution into Web 1.0 and Web 2.0, and now the proposed Web 3.0, the journey has been consistently fueled by both capital and technology, aiming to dismantle the monopolies established by previous technological eras. Hence, Web 3.0's emergence is a natural progression driven by the innovative impulses of capital and entrepreneurs seeking to forge new business models. Presently, this forthcoming transformation in business is what we're terming Web 3.0.

Innovation often requires technological advancements and capital infusion, making the pioneering spirit of investment a crucial component. In reaction to Web 3.0, prominent figures like Zhu Xiaohu of GSR Ventures explored novel ventures like buying sneakers from the game StepN, recognizing the economic model's potential. Meanwhile, venture capital giants like a16z (Andreessen Horowitz) and Sequoia Capital have backed numerous Web 3.0 initiatives.

By 2021, according to Techub News, the total investment in the Web 3.0 sector reached $29 billion, climbing to $33.2 billion by 2022.

The influx isn't limited to financial investments; technology and talent are also gravitating toward Web 3.0. Tech behemoths from Silicon Valley, including Meta, Google, Amazon, Twitter, and eBay, are delving into Web 3.0 explorations. For instance, Twitter's introduction of a feature displaying NFT profile pictures in a hexagonal shape marked its initial foray into Web 3.0. Similarly, Meta, YouTube, Reddit, and Google have announced plans to introduce NFT products, signaling their foray into Web 3.0.

Yet, the stark reality is that most current Web 3.0 projects do not fully embody the essence of Web 3.0 but hint at an upcoming wave of Internet technological transformation. This sentiment is widely acknowledged within the Web 3.0 community.

Take OpenSea, a platform often associated with Web 3.0; it operates with a Web 2.0 mindset, not fully embracing decentralization. While Web 3.0 is fundamentally about ownership—enabling users to truly own and control their digital assets—OpenSea and similar platforms fall short of providing a comprehensive cross-platform identity authentication system that would embody true Web 3.0 principles.

The Web 3.0 being discussed today is framed within our current technological landscape. However, with the advent of quantum computing and quantum communication, many of today's technologies will become obsolete, not adequately representing the real Web 3.0.

Moreover, the future vision of Web 3.0 leans toward de-platformization and collaborative cooperation, underscoring open-source, decentralization, and collaboration to foster a more inclusive and equitable digital economy. However, many current projects are entrenched in Web 2.0 ideologies, prioritizing their platform's independence over genuine decentralization. This misalignment is evident when projects vying for market dominance launch closed platforms without fostering interoperability and collaboration—underscoring the industry's deviation from a truly cooperative and mutually beneficial ethos.

Such cognitive constraints are understandable, given that industry participants, investors, and entrepreneurs are not futurists but are navigating through the limited technological advancements of today to carve out new business frontiers.

4.1.2 Web 3.0 and the Challenge of Overcoming Monopolies

The investment landscape in Web 3.0 is burgeoning, with industry titans like a16z, Sequoia Capital, and Bridgewater Associates diving into the arena, signaling a clear commitment to the future of Web 3.0. Yet, this investment fervor presents a paradox: while capital infusion can catalyze the growth and credibility of Web 3.0, its foundational mission—decentralization and user empowerment—clashes with traditional capital-driven paradigms prevalent in the Web 2.0 era.

This means that if capital seeks to build Web 3.0 platforms using its influence, these platforms are essentially still centralized, albeit constructed with a new technological concept that appears more open relative to Web 2.0. If a centralized platform cannot be established, capital cannot realize investment liquidation, valuation, returns, and exit strategies.

Reflecting on the Web 2.0 era, the business models of major Internet companies were based on centralizing platforms to attract traffic for monetization. Companies like Facebook (now Meta) and Twitter (now X), e-commerce platforms like Amazon and Taobao, and search engines like Google and Baidu relied on providing foundational services to attract user traffic for business monetization. The rise of these platforms was inseparable from capital support, with founders like Google's Larry Page and Sergey Brin, Facebook's Mark Zuckerberg, and Alibaba's Jack Ma receiving early boosts from capital.

However, the mission of Web 3.0 is decentralization and empowerment, which contradicts the traditional capital-driven model. In Web 3.0, users are granted more control, owning and managing their digital identities and data. This contrasts starkly with the centralized platform model of Web 2.0, which often monopolizes user data to achieve excessive returns. Web 3.0 aims to dismantle this monopoly, enabling users to directly benefit from their data, a radical shift from traditional business profit models.

Moreover, Web 3.0's decentralization allows users to directly benefit from their data, reducing dependence on centralized platforms. However, the traditional capital-driven business model seeks short-term monopolies and excessive returns, posing a core challenge for capital entering Web 3.0: how to balance business model innovation with capital return expectations. Capital's nature is to pursue monopolies, whereas Web 3.0 emphasizes dispersion and decentralization.

Despite claims of decentralization, objective reality suggests it's more an ideal than a practical reality—decentralization can only develop toward a more open and equitable direction with technological advancement, as ultimate control still resides with the platform's designers. To Elon Musk, current Web 3.0 appears more like a "marketing buzzword" than a reality.

Twitter co-founder Jack Dorsey argues that Web 3.0 will ultimately be controlled by venture capitalists, transitioning from one form of monopoly to another. Dorsey highlights that users don't truly own Web 3.0 products; instead, venture capital firms and their limited partners are the real owners, forever bound by their incentivization mechanisms. Ultimately, Web 3.0 may become a centralized entity under a different label. In the development of Web 3.0, investors might wield excessive influence through financial support, potentially turning Web 3.0 projects into tools for investors rather than truly decentralized networks serving users. Although Web 3.0's ethos emphasizes user ownership of data and digital assets, if ownership and decision-making remain centralized, users' genuine ownership rights are challenged.

Due to this contradiction, Jack Dorsey's project faced ostracism from its investors. In December 2021, Dorsey tweeted criticism of Web 3.0 as a tool for venture capital firms, leading to Marc Andreessen, founder of a16z, blocking him—a gesture Dorsey reciprocated. Dorsey's critique wasn't aimed at Web 3.0 itself but questioned whether investment methods were suitable—excessive venture capital involvement could result in Web 3.0 being dominated by capital, not citizens, contradicting Web 3.0's original intent.

While blockchain technology heralds a new era of more open and freer transactions, its promise of absolute security and decentralization is not without question. Take, for instance, the period before the FBI's intervention in Bitcoin-related activities. The broader community of virtual currency enthusiasts and blockchain experts held a firm belief in Bitcoin's untraceability and security. Yet, the FBI's ability to tackle Bitcoin-associated criminal activities challenged these assumptions, shedding light on potential vulnerabilities within the supposedly secure blockchain infrastructure.

At its core, Web 3.0 technology presents a significant advancement in enhancing information security and maintaining confidentiality. Nonetheless, in the realms of national governance and cybersecurity, absolute secrecy seems elusive. Government interventions or regulations could impinge on the decentralized nature of blockchain networks, potentially curtailing their autonomy. Despite the inherent transparency of blockchain, the technology is not immune to potential breaches or technical shortcomings, raising concerns about its infallibility.

The journey toward de-platformization, de-monopolization, and true decentralization in Web 3.0 is fraught with challenges. Should Web 3.0 fail to significantly distance itself from the centralization characteristic of its predecessor, it risks being dominated by capital influence, reducing it to a conceptually appealing yet practically hollow endeavor. In such a scenario, Web 3.0 might merely become another facet of digital currencies today—captivating in theory but potentially misleading, shaped by capital interests rather than genuine user empowerment and decentralization.

4.1.3 The Illusion of Decentralization

Centralization and its counterpart, decentralization, reflect the ongoing human quest for order and freedom within society. While we aspire to decentralized systems that offer greater autonomy and fairness, the inherent structure of human societies, reliant on order and governance, often necessitates a degree of centralization.

Centralization is intertwined with societal order, where governments and institutions lay down the rules and ensure their enforcement to maintain stability. This centralized approach is pivotal in coordinating societal interests, safeguarding the public good, and delivering swift responses in crises. However, this centralized efficiency presents obstacles to achieving true decentralization.

Decentralization champions a collaborative approach without a central authority, posing significant challenges, particularly in coordination and governance. Without a centralized entity, aligning diverse perspectives and interests becomes a formidable task, potentially leading to decision-making delays or conflicts. Additionally, the absence of a central authority might give rise to power imbalances, where decisions are swayed by dominant groups rather than a democratic consensus.

Moreover, decentralization's dispersal of power can introduce a degree of unpredictability and disorder, contrasting with the stability and clarity provided by centralized systems. The lack of a unified guiding authority can lead to a fragmented societal state characterized by conflicting interests and uncertain direction.

While decentralization aims for broader participatory decision-making, existing societal inequalities could skew this process, enabling more influential groups to disproportionately shape outcomes, thereby perpetuating or exacerbating existing disparities.

Ultimately, the concepts of centralization and decentralization revolve around how power and decision-making are distributed. While centralization focuses on a singular guiding authority for efficiency and unity, decentralization seeks to distribute this authority more broadly, albeit with challenges in achieving consensus and maintaining order. Despite the allure of a fully decentralized system, the complexity of societal governance and the need for coordination often necessitate a blend of both approaches, aiming for a balanced structure that can sustain and nurture societal growth and stability.

4.1.4 Reevaluating "Decentralization"

From a technological vantage point, attaining genuine decentralization is fraught with complexities. While the concept of Web 3.0 has sparked considerable interest across academia and industry, prevailing dialogues tend to be anchored in the tech paradigms of Web 2.0, with a heavy emphasis on blockchain as the bedrock of Web 3.0. Yet, for a more profound exploration of Web 3.0, it's crucial to transcend the limitations of present-day technologies and envisage Web 3.0 through the lens of emergent Internet technologies and state-of-the-art innovations.

Technological trends suggest that Internet technology based on blockchain is not the future of the Internet. The essence of blockchain does not represent decentralization but is a form of distributed ledger technology, a complex encryption technique that emerged as a necessity in the era of massive data proliferation. Although blockchain can achieve decentralization to some extent, it is not an absolute solution.

Blockchain originated as a response to trust and security issues in traditional centralized financial systems. The advent of Bitcoin marked a challenge against the monopolistic power of centralized financial institutions, aiming to establish a decentralized digital currency system. However, as blockchain technology evolved, it became apparent that decentralization is not the sole design choice for blockchain, and in some contexts, blockchain does not achieve true decentralization.

The inherent design features of blockchain technology limit its ability to achieve complete decentralization. In public blockchains, consensus mechanisms like PoW or proof of stake (PoS) do ensure some degree of decentralization. However, this does not equate to the entire blockchain network being fully decentralized. Some public blockchains exhibit high mining pool concentration, where a few large pools control most of the network's hashing power, leading to a new form of centralization. Moreover, private and consortium blockchains focus on controllability and efficiency, often adopting centralized management mechanisms in their initial design and practical applications.

This centralization tendency is evident not only in network structures but also in the demands of practical applications. To improve transaction speed and reduce costs, some blockchain projects introduce centralization elements by compromising on decentralization. For instance, consensus mechanisms tolerating Byzantine faults may sacrifice the decentralization of some nodes to ensure overall performance, a trade-off driven by business needs and performance optimization, sparking debates on the degree of blockchain decentralization.

Beyond the inability to guarantee decentralization, blockchain's security is increasingly questioned. Consensus mechanisms, the cornerstone of blockchain security, including PoW and PoS, aim to ensure that network nodes reach agreement on transactions and defend against potential attacks. However, if an entity controls more than 51% of the network's computational power, it could launch an attack on the blockchain system, known as a 51% attack.

In PoW, nodes compete to create blocks by solving complex mathematical problems, with nodes possessing more computational power and more likely to gain the right to create the next block. If an attacker controls over 51% of the computational power, they can create and control more blocks than other nodes, facilitating a double-spending attack. In PoS, the probability of a node being chosen to create a new block correlates with the amount of cryptocurrency it holds, requiring attackers to possess over 51% of the cryptocurrency to influence the system's consensus.

Small blockchain networks, due to their relatively fewer nodes and computational power, are more susceptible to 51% of attacks. Moreover, advances in quantum computing pose new challenges to traditional cryptographic algorithms. Blockchain networks predominantly use cryptographic algorithms like RSA and elliptic curve cryptography, which rely on mathematical problems that are difficult for current computer systems and offer relative security. However, emerging technologies like quantum computing could render these complex cryptographic algorithms obsolete.

RSA, based on the difficulty of factoring large integers, is widely used for secure communication and digital signatures. Shor's algorithm, a quantum computing-based algorithm, can efficiently solve the factorization of large integers, potentially compromising RSA's security. The advent of quantum computers could undermine RSA's safety by quickly solving this mathematical challenge.

Elliptic curve cryptography is another encryption algorithm used in blockchain, based on the discrete logarithm problem on elliptic curves, challenging for traditional computers but potentially solvable by quantum algorithms like Grover's.

In addition to 51% of attacks, blockchain faces challenges like smart contract vulnerabilities, network-level attacks, hard forks, and soft forks. Smart contracts' code quality directly impacts system security, with vulnerabilities exploitable by attackers. Network-level attacks, including DDoS and network partitioning, can cause delays, transaction failures, or node isolation. Hard forks and soft forks might lead to network splits and confusion, offering opportunities for potential attacks.

In summary, blockchain serves as a transitional technology in the evolution from Web 2.0 to 3.0. True Web 3.0 will likely not be based on blockchain but on advanced technologies like quantum computing, satellite technology, DNA storage, digital twinning, and more. Addressing the myriad challenges of decentralization, including technological, societal, and governance aspects, underscores the complexity of achieving true decentralization. While decentralization remains an aspirational goal reflecting humanity's quest for freedom, it's clear that as long as societal order and organizational structures exist, complete decentralization remains elusive.

In conclusion, the concept of decentralization in Web 3.0 is intertwined with the advancement of cutting-edge technologies and the reimagining of Internet infrastructure. However, the journey toward a fully decentralized web is fraught with technical, ethical, and practical challenges. As we venture into the potential of Web 3.0, it is imperative to critically evaluate the promises of decentralization against the backdrop of these challenges, recognizing that the future of the web may involve a blend of centralized and decentralized elements to cater to the diverse needs of a global digital society.

4.2 Reevaluating Web 3.0

In the current discourse, Web 3.0 finds itself at a crossroads. Advocates champion the original vision of the Internet as a space of unfettered openness, contrasting sharply with the monopolistic dominance of major Internet corporations. They propose Web 3.0 as a resurgence of the Internet's foundational principles, emphasizing a shift toward decentralization.

Yet, the decentralization heralded by blockchain technology remains elusive, more an ideal than an attainable reality. The inherent structures of governments and organizations within human societies impose a ceiling on how decentralized our systems can truly become—not just technologically but fundamentally, as a matter of societal organization.

Web 3.0, in many ways, mirrors the human quest for democracy: a principle universally aspired to yet perpetually contentious and elusive in its purest form. So, what is the true nature of Web 3.0? How can we accurately define it amid these debates?

4.2.1 The Core Issue with Web 2.0

The anticipation for Web 3.0 stems from long-standing grievances with Web 2.0, centered fundamentally around the issue of data ownership. In simpler terms, our rights to personal data have been unreasonably and ruthlessly stripped away.

Today, the value of data is indisputable, a result of Web 2.0's evolution. The rise of Web 2.0 marked the transition from a static information dissemination Internet to an era dominated by User-Generated Content, driving massive data generation, collection, and utilization, and highlighting the value of data.

In the Web 2.0 era, users transitioned from being mere consumers of the Internet to creators of content. Platforms like social media, blogs, and online forums enable users to easily share their thoughts, lives, and creativity, generating vast amounts of user-generated data that encapsulate interests, needs, and behavioral patterns.

This user-generated data became a valuable resource in the platform economy, enabling large tech companies to analyze user data for a better understanding of market trends, offering personalized services and targeted advertising, thus enhancing user experience and the commercial value of platforms. User data not only provides insights for businesses but also drives the development of AI and machine learning, expanding data's application fields.

This data-driven development model transformed the Internet into a vast information ecosystem, where various data interconnect, displaying complex network relationships. In this context, data serves not only as a commercial asset but also as a critical factor influencing societal operations, scientific research, and governmental decision-making.

Nowadays, the societal recognition and importance of data are unequivocal. Data, as a new factor of production, has rightfully earned its status. However, as data volume grows, data-related issues increasingly come into focus. Unlike any previous production resource, data reflects certain societal relations, making its utilization subject to externalities.

For instance, data related to users, their behaviors, and interactions between individuals touch upon privacy and personal information protection. Yet, in reality, data produced by users doesn't belong to them but is monopolized by centralized platforms. Furthermore, when we wish to use various platforms, they unilaterally demand our consent to relinquish our personal data in exchange for access rights. Once these platforms freely acquire our data, they misuse our behavioral data without our knowledge, leading to various issues like privacy breaches and data theft.

Take the example of ordering a boxed meal on a food delivery platform. After paying, the platform dispatches a delivery person, and once the order is complete, we not only receive a meal but also generate purchase data. This data includes our name, contact information, delivery address, spending amount, and food preferences. Although we created this data, we don't own it, can't exchange it for goods, nor does it bring us any benefits. Thus, for us, the data we created isn't an asset.

But what about the platform? Our behavioral data becomes a commodity for them. The platform might combine our data with that of hundreds or thousands of others in our vicinity, creating various rich dimensions for data processing, interpretation, and judgment. Based on this accumulated data, the platform knows how many delivery personnel to allocate in our area and what type of restaurants are most profitable here, and it uses our preferences to accurately recommend more products and advertisements. The platform can also commodify these data or accurately package the traffic and sell it to merchants on the platform for advertising. In this link, users are treated as "data cash cows," continually feeding platforms and businesses. In other words, if we are using a service for free, we are not the customer; we are the product itself.

Moreover, not only do we not own this data, but it can also pose risks to us. Imagine if the platform combines purchase data, delivery addresses, personal information, etc., of hundreds or thousands of users into a vast data set. By analyzing this data, the platform can gain deep insights into the consumption habits, demographic characteristics, and demand trends in users' areas. This provides valuable market intelligence for the platform, aiding in business strategy planning and resource allocation, but also poses potential risks to privacy security. If the platform's data security measures are inadequate, potential vulnerabilities go undetected and unpatched; this enormous data pool could become a target for hackers. They might employ various methods, including malicious software and social engineering, to access this data. Once successful, vast amounts of user personal information will be exposed, including names, contact information, and delivery addresses. This opens the door to identity theft, fraudulent transactions, and other malicious activities.

Data breaches can also lead to identity theft and phishing attacks. With users' real identity information, fraudsters can engage in various deceitful actions, including applying for loans or opening fake accounts. Moreover, through precise phishing attacks, attackers can masquerade as legitimate entities, enticing users to provide more sensitive information and leading to broader personal privacy breaches.

It's evident that personal data carries aspects of individual personality but is controlled by centralized platforms for their use. The increasing incidents of data breaches and misuse have awakened people's awareness of data security. The demand for individual control over personal data is intensifying, and people are starting to recognize the importance of individual data sovereignty.

Additionally, as technology propels society into a digital twin era, we are no longer purely biological beings but have derived a digital twin. In other words, we are no longer just physical entities but also digital ones in the digital realm. The emergence of digital twins will usher us into an era of digital sovereignty.

In the forthcoming era of digital twins, the concept of data sovereignty will increasingly come to the forefront. Individuals will recognize that their data, both personal and collective, transcends mere automated information, embodying distinct identities and rights. The advent of digital twins underscores the significance of data sovereignty, positioning each individual as a sovereign entity within the digital realm. This implies that we ought to possess and govern the rights to our personal information, behavioral data, and other digital imprints.

In light of this, the resistance against data monopolization by centralized platforms is a logical progression. There's a growing demand for a novel business paradigm that prioritizes technology and the user's perspective on data sovereignty. This is the core philosophy fueling the genesis of Web 3.0: an awakening to digital sovereignty and a revolt against the monopolization of data. Web 3.0 aims to radically alter the dynamics of data exchange, granting individuals enhanced control over their own data and transforming it from a commodity exploited by corporate behemoths to a means of individual and communal empowerment.

4.2.2 The True Web 3.0 Era

The core of Web 3.0 resides in the empowerment and sovereignty of individual digital identities, marking a significant shift and renaissance in human civilization. Web 3.0 signifies a move from traditional civil rights to a new realm where individuals exercise sovereignty over their virtual identities and actions in the digital domain.

In the digital landscape we've known, our digital identities have been somewhat passive, confined by the data monopolization and control exerted by centralized platforms. To access services, we've had to relinquish our data rights and authorize these platforms to manage and utilize our behavioral and privacy data. Consequently, our digital footprints are centrally stored and controlled, diluting our command over our digital selves. Centralized entities possess vast power over data and content rights, claiming ownership over user data and content, infringing significantly on individual data rights.

With the emergence of Web 3.0, a shift is on the horizon. Our digital identities will transform into sovereign entities, offering us more control over our data and identity information. This sovereignty allows for enhanced autonomy, enabling us to choose what data to share, with whom, and under what circumstances. It affords us the ability to manage our privacy more effectively, steering clear of unwarranted data collection and misuse. For instance, our selective data sharing during shopping can lead to tailored recommendations, while on social media, we can control who sees our activities and interests. In the financial domain, we gain the flexibility to choose services that align with our risk preferences and investment goals, moving beyond the one-size-fits-all approach of traditional institutions.

Moreover, we transition from mere data producers and consumers to active, independent entities within the digital realm. We can extract more value from our digital identities, actively engaging in the digital economy and contributing to a richer social fabric. Imagine a future where sharing an article on social media not only garners likes but also tangible rewards, as our content creation becomes a verifiable digital asset tied to our digital identity. This not only incentivizes quality content creation but also fosters a fairer value distribution mechanism, making the digital economy more equitable and inclusive.

Web 3.0 heralds a new era of digital sovereignty, envisioning a civilization that is more open, equal, and democratic. In this new era, every individual is a sovereign entity in cyberspace, with the autonomy to dictate their digital interactions. This freedom enhances information exchange, knowledge sharing, and participation in the digital economy and society, allowing for more dynamic management of digital identities.

In essence, Web 3.0 isn't just a technological leap; it's a pivotal moment in the evolution of society and civilization. Through digital sovereignty, individuals gain unprecedented control in the digital age, driving society toward a more open, equitable, and democratic future. This transformation reshapes not only individual roles in digital society but also the broader social, economic, and cultural landscapes, pushing human civilization forward in the digital age.

4.3 The Rise of Digital Identity

In modern society, identity serves as the gateway to handling tangible relationships and is the cornerstone for establishing and operating social order. Differentiating and authenticating tangible identity information and providing services that match the identity are crucial modalities in social relations.

However, with the advent and widespread adoption of the Internet, traditional concepts of identity have evolved, giving rise to a new form of expression: digital identity. Digital identity represents an individual's unique identifiers and characteristics in the digital space, distinct from traditional tangible identities and based on digital technology and network platforms.

Digital identity, too, has undergone a long developmental journey—from centralized identity to federated identity and now toward user-centric digital identity. Self-sovereign digital identity will emerge as the fundamental form of digital identity, encapsulating the essence of Web 3.0.

4.3.1 The Arrival of Digital Identity

Identity or subjectivity is defined through representation, self-representation, the categorization of identity, the connection between self and behavioral traits, and the approach to understanding "existence" in daily life. The construction of an individual's identity is influenced not only by physical traits but also by cultural, contextual, and social environmental factors.

From birth, everyone is endowed with a natural identity. This identity, shaped within specific languages, media, and cultures through categorizations or classifications, includes aspects like gender, race, ethnicity, class, sexual orientation, nationality, citizenship, educational background, socioeconomic status, and professional experience. These factors, combined with memory and experience, contribute to an individual's self-perception. Traditionally, a person's natural identity consists of physiological traits like gender and height, as well as social characteristics developed through interactions, such as profession, status, language, and beliefs.

Digital identity transcends mere physical characteristics, encompassing an individual's unique representation in the digital realm, akin to a digital "ID card." It's a concept that has gained prominence with the Internet's rise, signifying a shift from solely physical world identity representations to multifaceted digital personas.

The National Institute of Standards and Technology (NIST) in the United States defines digital identity as "the unique representation of a subject engaged in an online transaction." This encompasses attributes that uniquely identify individuals and their devices across various contexts, authenticating their legitimacy and specifying their access rights within digital systems.

In mainland China, an example of digital identity is the health code system, a preliminary version of a digital twin for individuals, intertwining personal information with public health efforts. Yet, it's an early stage in the evolution toward fully realized digital human twins. Digital twinning, in essence, creates a virtual, dynamic simulation of a physical entity, providing a comprehensive and interactive digital counterpart.

The health code, a pivotal tool during the pandemic, facilitated the integration of individual identity, travel, and health information, streamlining data verification processes and enhancing public health responses. It operates on a three-dimensional model, tracking spatial movements, temporal data, and interpersonal interactions to construct a detailed digital twin for each person.

Digital identity isn't confined to health applications; it's pervasive in our daily interactions, from using facial recognition for mobile payments to secure logins in corporate systems. This identity model incorporates an individual's online activities, social interactions, and data generation, painting a comprehensive digital portrait encompassing personal interests, relationships, and behaviors.

Thus, digital identity represents a fusion of real-world and virtual information, offering nuanced ways of recognizing and understanding individuals in a networked society. It heralds a new era where digital sovereignty empowers individuals, granting them control over their virtual presence and interactions in the digital age. This transformation signifies a major leap in the evolution of identity representation, aligning with the broader trajectory toward a more connected, interactive, and user-empowered digital future.

4.3.2 The Evolution of Digital Identity

The evolution of digital identity signifies its transformation from a mere representation of traditional identity into our "digital twin" in the virtual world. This evolution has been continuous, adapting to technological advancements.

In the early days of the Internet, the TCP/IP protocol was designed to provide communication identifiers for devices like computers, but it overlooked the need for a dedicated identity system for the people and organizations operating those devices. Consequently, makeshift identifiers such as IP addresses, MAC addresses, domain names, email addresses, phone numbers, and even product serial numbers were repurposed to serve as identifiers and proofs of identity for individuals and organizations. However, this lack of a reliable, built-in network-level identity system in the Internet's infrastructure made it easy for digital identities to be misused or hijacked, leading to identity leaks and thefts, forming the root cause of identity fraud, cybercrime, and privacy threats.

In the current digital landscape, the autonomy and transferability of digital identities, along with their distinctiveness and personal ownership, are pivotal. Without these elements, we face not only challenges with identity theft and privacy breaches but also hurdles in realizing the full potential of personal digital assets. As individuals increasingly interact in the digital world, leaving extensive digital footprints, the importance and value of these digital assets become more pronounced.

The evolution of digital identities can be delineated into four distinct phases: centralized digital identity, federated digital identity, user-centric digital identity, and self-sovereign identity (SSI). Among these, the SSI is not just the ultimate stage of digital identity evolution but also the ultimate vision that Web 3.0 aspires to achieve.

- **CENTRALIZED DIGITAL IDENTITY**

Centralized digital identities are managed and controlled by a single authoritative entity, and most digital identities on the Internet today are centralized. In this system, digital identities are inherently tied to specific organizations or platforms. Users lack control over their identity-related information and cannot determine who has access to their PII or the extent of that access. A user's digital identity can vanish or become invalid with the demise of the central organization or can be compromised due to poor management.

Taking the health code as an example, which serves as version 1.0 of the digital twin, it is issued and managed by governmental departments. In this centralized model, an individual user's digital identity data is stored on central servers, leading to a lack of agency in the usage and control of their identity information. Users can't decide who has access to their health code information or manage the extent of those access rights.

This centralization also raises the risks of individual privacy breaches. Since the central entity has absolute control over users' identity information, potential threats to personal privacy can arise from data breaches, abuse of authority, or improper access. While the sensitive nature of health information might make users more vigilant about their privacy, the inherent limitations of the centralized model could make users' health data susceptible to attacks or misuse.

In 2022, an incident erupted in Henan, China, where depositors at certain rural banks found their health codes inexplicably turned red. After a financial crisis at these rural banks, depositors intending to retrieve their savings or seek help from local regulatory bodies discovered their health codes had turned red without having visited any high-risk pandemic areas. Some depositors even received red codes without stepping foot in Henan, making the situation both clear and perplexing. Clearly, those assigned red codes were primarily the depositors affected by the bank crisis, seemingly unrelated to their actual movements. The perplexing part was the lack of clarity on who was assigning these red codes and how it was being done. The Henan Health Commission deferred to the city-level big data management bureau, which in turn pointed to the Zhengzhou Epidemic Prevention and Control Headquarters, which provided vague explanations.

In the context of centralized digital identities, the right to create, interpret, and store digital identities belongs to the identity service providers, while the right to use the identity is shared between the centralized institution and the user. Users must create completely independent digital identities for each application they use, managing multiple identities and keys. According to a survey by Penguin Intelligence, 14.9% of users use the same password for all their accounts. A Balbix report suggests that over 99% of users utilize the same password for multiple accounts. Similar scenarios are observed with the use of health codes; for example, when traveling to different cities, users may need to use different health codes managed by local governments, necessitating frequent switching and providing the same health information.

- **FEDERATED DIGITAL IDENTITY**

Federated digital identity emerged to address the challenges of centralized digital identity. The core idea behind federated digital identity is that multiple institutions or consortia jointly manage users' identity data. This collaborative management helps integrate and unify user identity information, addressing the fragmentation and chaos inherent in centralized identity management. Users' identity data are more completely and consistently managed, providing a more unified and clear digital identity.

Federated digital identity offers portability of user identity data, allowing users' identity information to flow freely among different federation members, not confined to a single platform. This means users can share their identity information more conveniently across various services and applications without the need to frequently recreate and verify their identities. Cross-platform login capabilities provided by QQ, WeChat, or Weibo are typical examples, where a single sign-on grants access to multiple platform services, enhancing the convenience of digital identity usage. Furthermore, federated digital identity enhances user interoperability, as a collaboration between multiple institutions or consortia ensures better coordination of user identity information across different systems and services. This interoperability not only makes users' digital identities more flexible but also offers a more comprehensive service experience.

While the federated digital identity model has succeeded in improving information integration, portability, and interoperability, it remains a centralized form of digital identity, often dominated by Internet giants, with limitations such as monopoly enterprises restricting single sign-on. Moreover, platforms typically need to recollect user information, reflecting a common issue in the Web 2.0 era, where centralized entities within the federation still hold absolute control over user identity data, leading to security and privacy concerns. Users still need to register and verify their identity within the federation, with the creation, interpretation, and storage rights of their digital identity remaining under the federation's control.

Against this backdrop, the concept of decentralized digital identity has emerged, offering a promising alternative to the centralized models.

4.3.3 Self-Sovereign Digital Identity

Decentralized digital identity represents a more advanced stage in digital identity management, primarily divided into two stages: user-centric digital identity and self-sovereign digital identity.

- **USER-CENTRIC DIGITAL IDENTITY**

User-centric digital identity focuses on decentralization, establishing an identity system centered around the user and attempting to grant users control over their digital identities. This is achieved through authorization and permission to share identity data. User-centric digital identity particularly emphasizes user authorization and interoperability, allowing users to share an identity across different services with their consent.

For instance, OpenID technology theoretically allows users to register and use their own OpenID independently. OpenID enables users to log in to various services and websites with a single identity, facilitating decentralized management of identity data and reducing reliance on centralized authorities. However, after the launch of OpenID in 2008, Facebook Connect achieved great success with a more user-friendly interface but deviated further from the user-centric concept, leading to increased monopolization.

- **SELF-SOVEREIGN DIGITAL IDENTITY**

Self-sovereign digital identity, however, represents true decentralization—complete ownership and control by the individual. It is the ultimate stage of digital identity management and the core concept pursued by Web 3.0. Under the SSI model, individuals fully own and control their digital identities without being subject to any centralized institutions or consortia. Individuals autonomously manage the creation, storage, verification, and sharing of their identities without third-party intervention. Self-sovereign digital identity empowers individuals to fully reclaim their identity, assets, and data, bringing them closer to the Internet dream of "efficiency, equity, trust, and value."

As a concept proposed by Penguin Intelligence, self-sovereign digital identity is based on a trust mechanism for identity management. This includes a method for identity and access management that allows individuals to generate, manage, and control their PII without the need for registrars, identity providers, or certifying authorities. PII comprises private, sensitive data that can be used to directly or indirectly identify an individual, typically including names, ages, addresses, appearances, citizenship, employment, and credit records.

In addition to PII, user-sovereign digital identity information also includes data from online electronic devices, such as usernames, passwords, search history, purchase history, etc. With a user-sovereign digital identity, users can control their PII by providing verification information. This identity management supports a trust mechanism that enables transparent and secure interactions.

The concept of SSI is central to the user's sovereign digital identity. Blockchain, Verifiable Credentials (VC), and DID are three key components of SSI. Blockchain is a decentralized digital database that provides a tamper-resistant and secure transaction ledger. VCs enable tamper-proof, secure, and credential verification, representing both physical credentials, like passports or licenses, and digital credentials without physical counterparts. DIDs are a new form of identifier, evolving from traditional centralized identities to emphasize decentralization and individual ownership and control.

In addition to the SSI rooted in blockchain, DID, and VC, the user-sovereign identity architecture includes four elements: the holder who creates a DID and receives a VC; the issuer who signs the VC with a private key and issues it to the holder; the verifier who checks the credentials and reads the issuer's public DID on the blockchain; and a user-sovereign digital identity wallet that powers the entire system.

In the future, digital identity construction will rely more on biometric technologies like facial, voice, or fingerprint recognition. This marks a more comprehensive and individualized stage in the evolution of digital identity. Compared to current DID technology, future digital identities built on biometric technology will be more convenient and secure.

In the DID model, users establish their identities through DID, emphasizing complete control and ownership over their identity data.

However, this model still relies on technologies like blockchain, requiring users to manage their digital identities. In contrast, biometric technology identifies individuals based on physiological or behavioral characteristics, offering a more convenient method of identity verification.

Moreover, biometric-based digital identities enhance security and convenience. Biological characteristics are unique and hard to forge, increasing digital identity security. Biometrics are harder to impersonate than traditional methods like usernames and passwords, reducing the risk of identity theft and fraud.

Self-sovereign digital identity envisions a future where data ownership equates to the choice of data monetization. In the past, platforms chose how to monetize user behavior or preferences data, treating users as products for profit. With data sovereignty, users regain the choice to sell their data or not. In Web 3.0, individuals become a part of the data market, connecting data producers and consumers, bringing profound changes to the digital society, and paving the way for a freer, more equal, and more democratic digital future.

CHAPTER 5

Actualizing Web 3.0

5.1 AI's Foundational Role in Web 3.0

Many have already felt the profound impact of AI on Web 2.0. For example, through deep learning and big data analysis, AI algorithms can accurately understand user behaviors, interests, and preferences, providing highly personalized content recommendations and services. Whether on social media platforms, e-commerce sites, or news apps, intelligent algorithms offer customized experiences. Search engines, using deep learning and natural language processing, deliver smarter and more precise search results, enhancing the user experience with more personalized and relevant outcomes.

In the Web 2.0 era, AI significantly influenced the entire Internet ecosystem, bringing optimizations and enhancements in various aspects. This influence of AI on the Internet ecosystem will extend into Web 3.0, injecting new vitality into it and even becoming a foundational technology for Web 3.0.

It can be said that AI technology is one of the key foundational technologies for Web 3.0. Without the integration of AI, achieving true Web 3.0 would be impossible. The core reason is that, with personal data becoming sovereign, combined with vast amounts of data generated by technologies like brain-computer interfaces and digital twins, the scale of data far exceeds human processing capabilities. Faced with this immense data complexity, we inevitably need the aid of AI to manage it effectively.

5.1.1 Deep Analysis of Massive Data

AI demystified can be likened to a digital brain that mimics human cognitive functions, where data acts as its knowledge base, algorithms as its thought processes, and computing power as its neural network's energy. At its core, AI employs sophisticated algorithms and powerful computational resources to deeply analyze, filter, process, and synthesize extensive data sets. Data is the bedrock upon which AI is built, and algorithms are its dynamic force driving innovation, and computing power is the indispensable catalyst.

Like human beings, AI needs to learn; however, instead of textbooks and classrooms, AI's education comes from data. It undergoes rigorous training with diverse datasets to acquire skills, discern patterns, and apply this knowledge to novel situations. Without a broad and rich data spectrum, AI's effectiveness and precision are severely limited.

Algorithms in AI are akin to complex problem-solving recipes, transforming raw data into insightful outcomes. They range from traditional machine learning frameworks to advanced neural networks, with deep learning standing at the forefront of AI's algorithmic evolution.

AI's prowess in decision-making, especially under uncertainty, heralds a new era of intelligence. Algorithms now predict renewable energy outputs, optimize industrial efficiencies, revolutionize retail strategies, and personalize digital experiences with unprecedented accuracy.

Turning to computing power, it's the backbone of AI's operational and training endeavors. The march of civilization has seen computational tools evolve from rudimentary counters to sophisticated AI processors. Mirroring the human brain's complexity, AI's computational demands are immense, necessitating robust hardware to match or even exceed human cognitive capabilities.

This trio of data abundance, algorithmic innovation, and formidable computing power enables AI to execute tasks with a precision and scale unattainable by humans alone, playing a pivotal role in shaping the Web 3.0 landscape.

5.1.2 The Necessity of AI in Web 3.0

The value of AI in Web 3.0 is readily apparent. Even in current contemplations of Web 3.0, based on Web 2.0 and blockchain technologies, AI remains a critical supporting technology.

In data analysis and intelligent decision-making, AI can provide Web 3.0 networks with more efficient and secure data analysis and intelligent decisions. For instance, AI can predict network demands by analyzing traffic data and improve network efficiency by dynamically adjusting resource configurations. Additionally, AI can enhance network security through data analysis. Twitterscan, a Web 3.0 AI platform that processes on-chain data, serves many individuals in the Web 3.0 realm, aiding them in understanding the latest projects and investment actions. It utilizes the on-chain data resources provided by Web 3.0 technology and the data analysis capabilities of AI to offer valuable information to users.

Smart contracts, automated programs that execute and record transactions based on blockchain technology, can be made more intelligent and flexible by AI in Web 3.0, enabling more complex business logic and transaction processes. AI can automate, program, and verify contracts by analyzing their content and optimizing and improving them by analyzing their execution results. Stability AI, an open-source AI company, uses blockchain technology to protect the ownership, privacy, and security of AI models, motivating AI developers and contributors through smart contracts. By leveraging the data security and incentive mechanisms provided by Web 3.0 technology, along with AI's intelligent modeling, Stability AI has created a new ecosystem in the AI domain.

Moreover, AI can develop more intelligent and user-friendly dApps for Web 3.0, enhancing user experience and value. AI can provide user recommendations, interactions, and services by analyzing user data and optimizing dApps through content analysis. Mirror, a decentralized blogging site built on Arweave, allows users to create, publish, and sponsor content with cryptocurrency, ensuring permanent and immutable content storage. Mirror utilizes the content ownership and storage mechanisms of Web 3.0 technology, along with AI's content analysis and recommendation capabilities, to offer a new creative platform for users.

Looking ahead, AI's more critical value in Web 3.0 lies in providing robust technical support for personal sovereign digital identities. Advanced data analysis algorithms enable AI to extract meaningful information from vast, complex personal data, precisely modeling digital identities. This is crucial for Web 3.0 development, as personal sovereign digital identities form the foundation of the digital society, representing individual identity and interests. AI's integration helps break traditional identity verification constraints, making digital identities more accurately and comprehensively reflect individuals' real characteristics.

AI also supports personalized services. Through deep analysis of personal data based on digital identities, AI can better understand individual interests, preferences, and habits, offering personalized intelligent assistant services. For example, by analyzing browsing history, social media activity, and purchase records, intelligent assistants can recommend products, services, or content suited to individuals' tastes and habits, improving personalized consumption experiences.

In data commodification, AI plays a crucial role. In the Web 3.0 era, data will become an important commodity and resource, with individuals and institutions benefiting from selling their data. AI helps individuals and institutions clean, filter, and package data in real-time, enhancing its commercial value. Additionally, AI's data analysis and prediction technologies help discover potential business opportunities and market demands, maximizing data utilization and value extraction.

In data security regulation, AI will also be significant. In the Web 3.0 era, data security will be a critical issue, with individuals and institutions needing to protect their data from intrusion and misuse. AI can ensure data security and privacy through encryption, privacy protection, and security monitoring techniques. Furthermore, AI can detect and respond to potential security threats and risks through real-time monitoring and analysis, ensuring data safety and trustworthiness in Web 3.0.

In conclusion, AI's value and impact in Web 3.0, characterized by personal sovereignty, are multifaceted. It not only provides technological means to construct digital identities but also strengthens advantages in personalization, security, and privacy protection, broadening the development prospects of personal sovereign digital identities in Web 3.0.

5.1.3 The Urgent Need for Web 3.0 in the Sora Era

On February 15, 2024, OpenAI officially released a product not known as GPT-5 but an AI model for generating videos called Sora. This marks the introduction of OpenAI's first text-to-video generation model, Sora, which is capable of creating detailed videos based on text prompts, extending existing video narratives, and generating scenes from static images. Essentially, if ChatGPT was confined to text generation, Sora would extend this capability to automatically generate corresponding video content based on an understanding of the human text.

Compared to text and image generation models, text-to-video generation models are more complex, requiring the model to accurately understand textual content and extract and generate corresponding visual content. Moreover, overcoming challenges such as data quality, computational power, and the complexity of integrated technologies is essential. Like ChatGPT, OpenAI's Sora demonstrated formidable capabilities upon its launch. OpenAI describes Sora as the foundation for understanding and simulating the real-world, viewing it as a significant milestone toward achieving AGI.

The industry's response to Sora has been overwhelmingly positive, with accolades like "explosive," "epic," and claims that "reality no longer exists." What makes Sora unique? Fundamentally, Sora is a text-to-video generation product that can create movie-like realistic scenes based on brief or detailed prompts or a static picture featuring multiple characters, various actions, and intricate backgrounds. Essentially, inputting a sentence prompts AI to generate a corresponding video segment.

In the 48 demonstration videos released by Sora, two examples vividly showcase its capabilities. For instance, AI's imagination of the Chinese Lunar New Year's festival features bustling crowds, curious children watching dragon dance troupes, and many people taking photos, depicting numerous characters engaging in diverse activities.

Sora's capabilities exceed those of existing AI video models like Runway and Pika in several ways. First, it significantly extends video length beyond the 10-second limit of previous models, reaching over 60 seconds. Second, it offers more stable video content, achieving multi-angle shot transitions within a single video and maintaining coherence and realism.

Last, its deep language comprehension allows for rich expressions and vivid emotions in generated videos, demonstrating an understanding of the physical world's rules.

Technologically, Sora's success is attributed to a novel architecture—the diffusion Transformer model, which combines features of diffusion and autoregressive models. OpenAI's approach to training video models uses visual patches, slicing videos and images into smaller blocks and compressing them into a low-dimensional space. This process starts with videos resembling static noise, progressively removing noise to transform it into coherent videos.

If 2023 marked the year of large language models, 2024, driven by OpenAI's Sora, heralds the era of AI-generated videos. Sora's breakthrough in hyper-realistic AI-generated video technology poses profound implications for human knowledge acquisition, learning modalities, and societal impacts. With Sora's capability to generate highly realistic videos, combined with ChatGPT's advanced text generation, AI will dominate information dissemination, influencing human cognition fundamentally.

Before Sora's emergence, humanity was already navigating the complexities of the Web 2.0 era, with algorithms significantly shaping individual and collective perceptions. The advent of Sora intensifies these challenges, necessitating a transition to true Web 3.0. In a data-sovereign Web 3.0 world, every piece of data, whether from humans, objects, or AI, will be tagged, clarifying ownership and provenance. This transparency will empower us to discern the origins of AI-generated content, maintaining a clear boundary between human and machine-generated information and aiding in the preservation of human autonomy in the age of algorithms.

5.2 Quantum Computing: Disruption and Foundation in Web 3.0

When contemplating the future of Web 3.0, blockchain and quantum computing stand out as two highly focal and debated technologies. At present, the vision for Web 3.0 is largely constructed on the foundation of blockchain technology. However, I contend that advancements in quantum computing could precipitate blockchain's decline, as quantum computing holds the capability to decrypt the most sophisticated blockchain encryption methods. This perspective seemingly casts quantum computing as an antagonist within the Web 3.0 landscape.

At its core, blockchain represents an advanced encryption methodology devised to bolster data security in the big data era. Therefore, it's accurate to describe blockchain technology as both essential and transitional for this era. I firmly believe that the genuine inception of Web 3.0 will not be anchored in blockchain's decentralized technology but will usher in a new era of decentralization driven by quantum computing and quantum communications.

Indeed, if we adopt a perspective grounded in the forefront of technological evolution to consider Web 3.0, the relationship between quantum computing and Web 3.0 is not inherently adversarial. While blockchain may not underpin the future Web 3.0, quantum computing has the potential to actualize true decentralization of computational power. Quantum communication promises unparalleled security that is theoretically unbreakable, positioning it to play an indispensable role in the era of Web 3.0.

5.2.1 Quantum Computing and the Evolution of Blockchain

Quantum computing has become a focal point in cutting-edge technology fields, representing a significant exploratory direction for the exponential advancement of computational power. With its potential to far exceed classical computing in parallel processing, quantum computing is poised to revolutionize numerous sectors.

Unlike classical computers that use bits as the unit of information, quantum computers utilize qubits. Qubits can represent both "0" and "1" simultaneously, thanks to their superposition property. This characteristic allows quantum computers to process a vast array of combinations at once, making them exponentially faster in certain tasks than their classical counterparts.

The most cited example is prime factorization. While classical computers take an enormous amount of time to factorize large numbers, quantum computers can achieve this in seconds using algorithms like Shor's algorithm. The profound computational capabilities of quantum computers signify a groundbreaking shift in technology, likened in importance to the Manhattan Project of the last century.

How does quantum computing threaten blockchain? The essence of blockchain is its robust security and reliability. Bitcoin, one of the most renowned applications of blockchain technology, utilizes cryptographic methods like hash functions and asymmetric cryptography for mining and digital signatures.

Quantum computing poses a significant threat to these cryptographic foundations. Quantum algorithms, such as Shor's algorithm, could potentially decrypt hash functions and asymmetric cryptography, undermining the security backbone of blockchain systems like Bitcoin. If a quantum computer can quickly solve these cryptographic challenges, it could monopolize the blockchain, fundamentally compromising its integrity.

The emergence of quantum computing indicates that the security and reliability blockchain technology prides itself on could be shattered. If blockchain's cryptographic underpinnings are vulnerable to quantum attacks, the envisioned Web 3.0 based on blockchain might face insurmountable challenges.

In conclusion, while blockchain technology is a key player in the current Web 3.0 narrative, the rise of quantum computing necessitates a reevaluation of the foundational technologies that will underpin the future digital era. The interplay between blockchain and quantum computing will undoubtedly shape the evolution of Web 3.0, urging a shift toward a quantum-powered decentralized future.

5.2.2 Decentralized Computing with Quantum Technology

The concern that quantum computing and Web 3.0 are at odds with each other likely won't materialize. Contrary to common apprehension, blockchain isn't the future of Web 3.0. From an advanced technological standpoint, quantum computing is essential for realizing a Web 3.0 era defined by self-sovereign digital identities.

- **DECENTRALIZED COMPUTING UNLEASHED BY QUANTUM TECHNOLOGY**

Quantum computing promises true decentralization in the Web 3.0 era. Traditional computing relies on centralized data centers and cloud providers. Users must access these centralized servers to obtain computing resources and process data.

This reliance on centralized computing is primarily due to the limited computational power at the user end. For example, despite the considerable processing power of the most advanced smartphones, they are incapable of handling vast data storage and processing requirements. With quantum technology, individuals could potentially perform most computing tasks on their own devices without relying on centralized servers or cloud services.

This shift empowers individuals with greater control and autonomy. They can perform high-performance computations on their devices without sending data to external servers, reducing potential risks and security concerns during data transmission.

- **ENABLING END-TO-END DATA CONNECTIVITY AND INTERACTION**

Quantum computing could also facilitate direct end-to-end data connectivity and interaction. Traditional data exchanges usually require centralized servers for routing and processing, which could compromise data security due to third-party control. However, with powerful quantum computing capabilities, individuals can engage in data interactions directly without relying on centralized servers.

This direct interaction model minimizes the risk of data being tampered with, stolen, or surveilled during transmission. It ensures a higher level of security and privacy for data exchanged between users or devices.

- **IMPLICATIONS FOR WEB 3.0**

Quantum computing will play a crucial role in realizing true decentralization in Web 3.0. It will not only enable decentralized computing power but also support direct, secure end-to-end data connections. As quantum chip technology evolves, every intelligent terminal could become a supercomputer in its own right, heralding an era of truly decentralized computing power.

In conclusion, understanding quantum computing's significance from a forward-thinking perspective reveals its pivotal role in shaping a Web 3.0 world. It will not only disrupt traditional computing paradigms but also pave the way for a decentralized, secure, and user-empowered digital future.

5.3 Quantum Communication: Transforming the Future of Connectivity

At the heart of the Internet's utility is its capacity for communication, and while current protocols and technologies have substantially advanced global connectivity, several core challenges—such as interoperability, data sovereignty, and privacy—still hinder the digital era from reaching its full potential.

Blockchain technology has been viewed as a beacon of hope, offering prospective solutions to these pressing issues. Yet, the swift advancements in quantum computing have cast a shadow over the security and reliability that blockchain purports to offer.

In this evolving scenario, quantum communication steps into the limelight. It is anticipated that critical concerns surrounding interoperability, data ownership, and privacy will be addressed. Furthermore, by embodying a decentralized framework, quantum communication could empower users with unprecedented control over their data, heralding a new era of secure, transparent, and user-centric digital communication.

5.3.1 Persistent Communication Challenges

Bound by the technical limitations of traditional communication, issues like interoperability, data ownership, and privacy security have always been problematic for the communication industry. These issues also pose technical barriers to transitioning from Web 2.0 to 3.0.

Interoperability refers to the seamless ability of different systems, platforms, or devices to communicate, exchange data, and share resources. It usually involves the interaction of different software, hardware, or network devices, allowing them to work effectively together to achieve a certain function or goal. For instance, a gaming PC typically consists of components produced by various manufacturers and software companies, yet they work cohesively as a whole. In the digital era, interoperability is key to enabling seamless connections and cooperative work among different systems, platforms, and devices, aiding in the sharing and circulation of information and enhancing system flexibility and scalability.

However, based on traditional communication technology, achieving interoperability is often challenging. The lack of unified standards and communication protocols is one of the root causes of interoperability issues. Due to the absence of standardized data formats and communication protocols, exchanging data and communicating between different platforms become difficult. For example, a social media platform might use a specific data format to store user information, while an e-commerce platform might use a completely different format. To facilitate data exchange between these two platforms, complex data conversion and mapping are required, complicating development and integration.

Moreover, technical differences between digital platforms contribute to interoperability issues. Different platforms may use varying programming languages, database technologies, and network protocols, leading to differences in system architecture and data processing methods. These differences complicate data exchange and communication between platforms, increasing the difficulty of integration and collaboration.

Data ownership is another long-discussed issue in the Web 2.0 era. In current communication services, users typically need to accept service terms when utilizing various services. These terms may authorize service providers to collect, store, process, and share user data. Since these terms are often articulated in complex and lengthy legal terminology, users struggle to fully understand their content, making it difficult to accurately assess how their data is used and the associated risks. This situation leads to ambiguity and obscurity regarding data ownership, where users' control over their data diminishes significantly. Data usage and circulation often occur beyond users' direct control, easily resulting in data misuse or privacy infringement.

With data ownership unclear and users unable to grasp how their data is used and circulated, privacy protection is even more elusive.

The emergence of blockchain technology has offered hope, forming the basis of current expectations for the future Web 3.0. Developers can use blockchain to create on-chain messaging and interconnection methods, relying on peer-to-peer network protocols for message transmission. Blockchain appears to be a promising method to address these communication challenges.

However, blockchain has its drawbacks, including the lack of real-time communication, decentralization, and network latency. Blockchain's real-time communication capabilities are limited, and message transmission is slow, mainly due to the inherent characteristics of blockchain's design architecture and consensus mechanisms. In the blockchain network, each node needs to verify and record transactions and reach a consensus through the consensus algorithm, causing delays and reduced speed in message transmission. Especially in scenarios with large-scale transactions, the performance of the blockchain network may be severely affected, hindering fast message transmission and processing.

The decentralized nature of blockchain could also contribute to network latency issues. Although decentralization enhances data security and credibility, it introduces complexity and delays in communication between nodes. Since data must be transmitted and verified across multiple nodes, the communication process could become slow and unstable. Particularly when the network is heavily loaded or when nodes malfunction, the latency issues in the blockchain network might become more pronounced, affecting the efficiency and reliability of communication.

Additionally, the current blockchain is fundamentally built on complex encryption algorithms, and the multi-ledger mechanism increases data space occupancy, leading to unnecessary resource wastage. Every node needs to store a complete copy of blockchain data, resulting in storage resource waste and increased data redundancy. Especially as the blockchain network expands and data volume grows, this resource wastage issue could intensify, affecting the network's performance and scalability.

5.3.2 A Technology to Transform the Future of Communication

While blockchain technology offers new perspectives and possibilities for addressing traditional communication challenges, it's evident that blockchain is not perfect and still faces many limitations and technical issues. In fact, from the perspective of communication technology evolution, the technology that truly has the potential to revolutionize the communication industry is quantum communication.

Quantum communication is a new type of communication method that uses quantum entanglement to transmit information. Quantum entanglement is a mysterious and profound phenomenon in quantum mechanics, describing a strange connection between two or more quantum particles where their states are interdependent, even when separated. This means observing one particle instantaneously influences its entangled counterpart, regardless of the distance between them. However, quantum entanglement only occurs within quantum systems and does not exist in classical mechanics. For example, if a fundamental particle with zero spin decays into two particles with opposite spins, measuring one particle's spin direction instantly reveals the other's opposite spin direction.

Theoretically, quantum entanglement can occur regardless of distance, meaning measuring one particle's state instantly reveals the other's, even if they are at opposite ends of the universe. This instantaneous connection surpasses conventional physical theories and is not limited by the speed of light, enabling instant information transmission.

Quantum communication doesn't directly transmit information through quantum entanglement but uses quantum's unique properties of being unclonable and undergoing measurement collapse to theoretically ensure absolutely secure encryption, something no current communication technology can achieve. This is quantum communication's greatest advantage.

In classical physics, replicating a bit's state (0 or 1) is straightforward. However, in quantum mechanics, the no-cloning theorem dictates that attempting to copy an unknown quantum state inevitably alters the original, leading to "measurement collapse."

Due to quantum's unclonability, attackers cannot replicate transmitted quantum bits without detection. Even if an attacker intercepts quantum bits, they cannot clone them for further surveillance or analysis. Quantum's measurement collapse ensures that any attempt to measure or interfere with quantum bits during transmission causes quantum entanglement collapse.

Incorporating entangled quantum particles into electromagnetic wave information allows the detection of eavesdropping attempts through triggered quantum collapse, alerting both sender and receiver to cease transmission. Eavesdroppers triggering this collapse gain no valuable information from the transmission process.

Compared to traditional communication methods, which focus primarily on reliable data transmission without emphasizing security, quantum communication heralds a new era in secure communication. Traditional communication often relies on encryption techniques to safeguard information, but with the advent of quantum computing, many of these encryption methods could easily be compromised. Quantum computing's parallel processing capabilities pose a significant threat to current encryption technologies, making once-secure data vulnerable.

In conventional cryptography, plaintext is the term for the original message that needs to be securely transmitted. This plaintext is converted into ciphertext through a process called encryption, and the reverse process is known as decryption. The rules used during these processes are known as keys. Modern communication commonly uses computer algorithms as these keys. Symmetric encryption, an early cryptographic method, uses the same key for both encryption and decryption, which, although effective and technically mature, poses a significant risk in key transmission.

To ensure communication security, the key must be securely transmitted to the receiver through a secondary channel. If intercepted, the communication's content becomes vulnerable. This challenge in key transmission led to the development of asymmetric encryption technology, which is heavily utilized in the blockchain. Asymmetric encryption involves each communication participant having a pair of keys: a public key for encryption and a private key for decryption. The encryption algorithm is public, but the decryption algorithm remains secret. Due to this asymmetry, asymmetric encryption technology was born.

One of the most popular asymmetric encryption algorithms is the RSA algorithm, named after its inventors Ron Rivest, Adi Shamir, and Leonard Adleman. The RSA algorithm relies on the difficulty of factoring the product of two large prime numbers. While it's easy to multiply two primes, factoring their product is much more challenging, especially as the numbers grow larger.

For classical computers, cracking high-bit RSA encryption is nearly impossible. However, a quantum computer using Shor's algorithm could easily break RSA encryption in seconds, presenting a significant threat to information security. Consequently, if we aim to ensure communication security in the Web 3.0 era, quantum communication will be crucial.

Moreover, blockchain-based communication faces issues like resource wastage due to its multi-ledger mechanism. Each node in a blockchain network stores a complete copy of blockchain data, which increases storage requirements as the network and data grow. For example, the data size of public blockchains like Bitcoin and Ethereum is enormous, posing a significant storage challenge for nodes.

Quantum communication doesn't have this problem. Quantum teleportation (QT), a feature of quantum communication, allows direct information transfer without transmitting actual quantum bits. Unlike traditional data transmission, which often involves copying and transmitting data bits, QT leverages quantum entanglement and measurement principles to transmit information directly to the target node, avoiding redundancy and reducing resource needs.

Compared to traditional or blockchain technologies, quantum communication offers clear advantages in security, speed, capacity, latency, and stability. As quantum communication technology continues to evolve, it's anticipated that it will replace traditional communication methods in the Web 3.0 era, becoming the primary communication infrastructure for the digital society of the future.

5.4 DNA Storage: The Storage Future of Web 3.0

As we enter the Web 3.0 era, the concept of data is undergoing a transformative shift. This new digital age, underscored by the emphasis on personal data sovereignty, anticipates individuals generating vast amounts of data spanning various facets of life, including personal interests, professional activities, social engagements, and health metrics.

This burgeoning data growth necessitates a parallel increase in storage solutions. Traditional storage methods, whether centralized systems reliant on hard disk drives or decentralized blockchain-based solutions are increasingly strained under the weight of this data deluge. In this context, reimagining data storage is not just beneficial but essential for the seamless operation and realization of Web 3.0's potential.

One innovative approach that stands out in this scenario is DNA storage. This cutting-edge technology offers a compelling solution to the storage challenges posed by Web 3.0, providing a way to store vast amounts of data in a compact, durable, and efficient format. With DNA storage, data is encoded into the building blocks of life, offering a paradigm shift in how we conceive and manage data storage for the future, ensuring that the infrastructure of Web 3.0 is as revolutionary as its promise.

5.4.1 Evolution of Storage Technology

From magnetic tapes to USB drives, various storage media have been developed over the years. However, today, an increasing amount of data is stored in data centers. Currently, there are about 10 exabytes (10 billion gigabytes) of digital data on earth, and every day, humans produce approximately 2.5 quintillion bytes of data through emails, photos, tweets, and other digital files. Most of this data is stored in massive facilities known as exabyte data centers, which can span the size of several football fields. Yet, a large data center capable of storing 1 billion GB can occupy the area of multiple football fields and cost up to $1 billion to construct and maintain. Thus, storing these vast amounts of data requires significant space and financial resources. Moreover, the rate at which data is generated far exceeds the pace of storage medium production, indicating a pressing need for more storage space, as current methods are falling short.

Furthermore, the prevailing storage solutions, primarily hard disk drives or cloud storage services, are predominantly centralized, meaning data is concentrated in a few large data centers or servers managed by cloud service providers. These platforms are willing to bear the high storage and operational costs because they own the massive data pools and can leverage them to offer various value-added services to users, thereby generating profits.

However, the drawbacks of centralized storage are apparent, including notorious privacy risks and security issues. Data centralized in a few nodes is vulnerable to loss or leakage if a fault occurs or if the system is attacked. Moreover, data exchange and access are contingent on authorization and management by centralized platforms, limiting users' control over their data and data sovereignty. Centralized storage models are also susceptible to surveillance and intervention by regulatory bodies and third-party organizations, potentially compromising user privacy and data security.

To address these privacy and security issues, decentralized storage has emerged as a solution, aligning with the ongoing development of Web 3.0. The current phase of Web 3.0 development is driven by distributed blockchains, which offer greater accessibility to cloud storage without compromising security. In the Web 3.0 storage paradigm, files are stored across a computer network rather than on a single server. With no central authority controlling the platform, users can freely choose their storage providers, such as Storj, IPFS, Ankr, Filecoin, and Arweave, each with its advantages and disadvantages.

- **IPFS: A CORNERSTONE OF DECENTRALIZED STORAGE IN THE WEB 3.0 ECOSYSTEM**

IPFS is a cornerstone technology in the decentralized storage domain, pivotal to the architecture of Web 3.0. It empowers individuals to set up their IPFS node, facilitating a global network where users can store data.

This system's appeal lies in its open and no-cost entry, allowing users to connect and share data without the need for formal registration and democratizing data storage.

However, the principle that there are no free lunches applies here as well. When a file is uploaded to an IPFS node, it remains on that node unless actively duplicated elsewhere. This mechanism places the onus of data redundancy on the network's nodes, which, without explicit incentives, rely on altruistic cooperation—a challenging foundation for sustainable data availability. Popular data benefits from network caching, becoming more accessible as it's requested across the network, but less popular or rarely accessed data might not be replicated sufficiently, posing risks of data loss or unavailability.

The rise of NFTs has thrust IPFS into the spotlight, with many seeing it as an ideal solution for storing NFT metadata due to its decentralized nature. Yet, the question remains: What happens when the sole node storing vital data goes off-line? While IPFS distributes data across various nodes, enhancing resilience and reducing the risk of data loss, the data's persistence is only as strong as the network's weakest link—if all nodes storing a piece of data go off-line, that data becomes inaccessible.

Therefore, while IPFS presents a groundbreaking approach to decentralized storage, reflecting the ethos of Web 3.0, it is not without its vulnerabilities. The potential for single-point failures underscores the necessity for comprehensive backup strategies and incentivization mechanisms to ensure data longevity and reliability, particularly for critical data like NFT metadata. Ensuring data persistence in the IPFS network requires a thoughtful approach to node redundancy and incentivization, reinforcing the network's foundational promise of decentralized, resilient storage.

- **FILECOIN: THE INCENTIVE LAYER OVER IPFS**

Recognizing the incentive deficit in IPFS, Protocol Labs introduced Filecoin, a complementary network that infuses economic stimuli into the IPFS ecosystem. Filecoin inaugurates a marketplace for storage, where network participants, dubbed miners, earn compensation for offering storage capacity and retrieval bandwidth, engaging in what is known as storage deals.

This introduces a predicament commonly encountered in the realm of digital storage: if an NFT creator ceases storage fee payments, their data faces purging. NFT proprietors are left without recourse or warning in such scenarios. Filecoin's integration into user-centric applications presents challenges, particularly for front-end applications, a staple in many Web 3.0 projects, despite its backend compatibility.

- **ARWEAVE: A BLOCKCHAIN-BASED STORAGE SOLUTION**

In contrast to IPFS and Filecoin, Arweave adopts a blockchain framework, thereby embodying the inherent blockchain virtues of immutability and perpetual data retention. Its economic model incentivizes miners to store and maintain a comprehensive replica of the Arweave blockchain. Arweave offers a compelling proposition with its one-time payment for what is effectively permanent storage, setting it apart from Filecoin's recurring cost model. Moreover, data retrieval on Arweave is significantly swifter compared to the process on Filecoin, which, despite leveraging IPFS for quicker access, still incurs notable delays.

Nonetheless, Arweave isn't exempt from blockchain-specific challenges, such as block times, which influence the pace of data uploads and interactions on the network. While Arweave's block time is relatively moderate compared to other blockchains, it can still impact the user experience, particularly for smaller data uploads.

Furthermore, Arweave's requirement for users to provide their private keys for data uploads introduces a layer of security consideration, necessitating vigilant management of sensitive credentials to mitigate potential risks.

In the quest for a Web 3.0 that champions true user sovereignty and digital identity, the exploration for innovative storage solutions continues, seeking to transcend the limitations and challenges posed by the current offerings in the decentralized storage domain.

5.4.2 The Value of DNA Storage

In the era of Web 3.0, as decision-making information and data affirming personal sovereignty increasingly go digital, the demand for storage is projected to skyrocket. Yet, existing storage technologies—both centralized and decentralized—grapple with challenges such as high costs, data security, and reliability. In response, the spotlight is turning toward a more sophisticated form of biological storage: DNA storage technology.

The hallmark of DNA storage is its astounding information density. To put it into perspective, the human genome, with its complexity and richness, stores about 750 MB of data in a strand of DNA smaller than a cell, meticulously orchestrating everything from the placement of our noses to the color of our eyes.

At the core of DNA are four nucleotides—adenine, guanine, cytosine, and thymine—forming a linear sequence that efficiently encodes life's blueprints. This system is not unlike our daily communication with words and sentences or the binary sequences computers use, only that DNA's alphabet is quartet-based instead of binary.

This digital-like encoding is highly translatable across various systems, reminiscent of how cells translate DNA into RNA and then into proteins—a process of genetic information conversion into action that's seamless and unmatched by any human-made system.

DNA is inherently information-rich, making it a more intuitive storage medium compared to traditional methods requiring physical media. This understanding has propelled scientists to devise ways to encode and store information in DNA, harnessing its stability and compactness for data retention.

Moreover, DNA's ability to store information with negligible degradation was highlighted in 2019 when scientists created a plastic rabbit embedded with DNA data, demonstrating DNA's potential for high-fidelity and long-term information storage.

Globally, the data generated annually would necessitate 418 billion 1 TB hard drives for storage. In stark contrast, this data could be stored in just 1 kg of DNA material, enduring up to a million years at −18°C. While paper decays and hard drives degrade, DNA's resilience offers a timeless vault for humanity's knowledge and history.

DNA's virtues as a storage medium—its compactness and stability over millennia—herald a new dawn in data storage, promising immense data capacity within minimal physical space and with longevity that traditional storage mediums can scarcely fathom. This shift not only signifies a leap in cost-efficiency but also marks a move toward sustainability, as DNA storage obviates the need for large-scale data centers and their associated upkeep, relying instead on the natural stability and efficiency of DNA molecules.

As we transition from Web 2.0 to 3.0, where data sovereignty becomes paramount, the need for personal accountability in data storage becomes evident. DNA storage emerges as a compelling solution, offering low-cost, high-security, and vast-capacity storage. This technology paves the way for a future where dependence on large data centers diminishes, allowing individuals and organizations to take charge of their data through their own storage nodes.

In addition, DNA storage ensures unparalleled data security and reliability. Its inherent stability and resistance to interference safeguard against data loss or corruption, while its distributed nature mitigates risks of centralized points of failure. The high density of DNA storage also means that a vast amount of data can be stored in a minuscule physical space, enhancing the security and reliability of data while reducing the complexity and footprint of storage infrastructure.

In essence, DNA storage technology is poised to be a cornerstone in the evolution of Web 3.0 storage solutions, offering a glimpse into a future where our vast data storage needs could be met by just a few cells' worth of DNA, securely preserving our digital legacy for millennia to come.

—CHAPTER 6—

Web 3.0 in Shaping Future Business Transformations

6.1 Disrupting Web 2.0: The Web 3.0 Revolution

The swift evolution of groundbreaking technologies such as AI, quantum computing, quantum communications, and DNA storage positions us at a pivotal junction of the digital era. As Web 3.0 emerges, it's incubating a radically new commercial landscape.

In the Web 2.0 era, users have been relegated to mere data producers, minuscule components in vast pools of traffic, with their value monopolized by centralized platforms. Web 3.0, however, signals a monumental shift. When data ownership transitions from centralized entities back to the creators—the users—it not only heralds a technological transformation but also promises to overturn the prevailing business paradigms, reshaping the commercial and economic structures of tomorrow.

6.1.1 The Core of Web 2.0 Business Models

Web 2.0 has been dominated by the platform economy, where the core strategy involves accumulating extensive user data and capitalizing on it. In layman's terms, it's about converting traffic into cash.

Yet, this model fosters a significant challenge: monopoly. Platforms' control over user data forms the bedrock of the platform economy, nurturing a breeding ground for monopolistic practices. Centralized data storage in Web 2.0 endows platforms with undue control over user data, cementing their monopolistic stature. Moreover, within the centralized Web 2.0 framework, users must navigate through Internet platforms to interact, storing their personal and behavioral data in centralized repositories, thereby relinquishing control over their data.

In essence, Web 2.0 platforms are naturally predisposed toward monopolistic tendencies due to their inherent technological design. The addition of a new user incurs negligible costs, yet potentially enriches the platform's value. For instance, the more individuals use WeChat Pay, the more valuable it becomes for both consumers and merchants, driving a virtuous cycle of adoption.

In this realm, platforms experience escalating returns to scale. Unlike traditional businesses, which rely on consumable resources with non-zero marginal costs, platforms operate differently. One user's participation doesn't detract from another's experience or add to the company's overhead, enabling platform-based enterprises to unleash a potency unmatched by traditional models. This escalating scale effect, or "network effect," intensifies as the user base expands. Social platforms like Facebook or WeChat grow as they attract more users, creating high switching costs and solidifying user loyalty. E-commerce platforms exhibit similar dynamics, where an abundance of merchants draws more consumers, which in turn attracts more vendors, fostering a robust cross-side network effect. Once a platform surpasses a critical mass, it often becomes the de facto choice, marginalizing potential competitors.

Today's leading platforms have evolved into sprawling, deeply entrenched ecosystems. Giants like Alibaba and Tencent command trillion RMB valuations, dominating our digital interactions. Our smartphones are portals to their expansive realms, with apps like WeChat, Sina Weibo, Pinduoduo, Meituan, and Tmall becoming daily staples. These platforms, with their vast user bases and deep-rooted networks, exemplify the entrenched power dynamics shaping the digital landscape, a testament to the transformative potential awaiting in the era of Web 3.0.

6.1.2 The Consequences of Platform Monopolies

Today, major Internet platforms have crafted extensive commercial ecosystems across various domains through business expansion, investments, and acquisitions. They've consolidated user data from diverse digital realms such as social media, shopping, transportation, and healthcare, setting the stage for further market expansion. The monopolistic nature of these Internet behemoths is particularly aggressive. Unlike traditional companies that vie for market share, these platforms compete for the market itself, ushering in a host of issues.

From a business standpoint, when the market is highly concentrated among a few platform-based enterprises, these platforms gain significant control over pricing, discourse, and rule-setting, leading to a winner-takes-all scenario. For instance, Apple's imposition of a 30% fee on in-app purchases, the so-called "Apple tax," increases the overall cost for users. Yet, established usage habits and high switching costs bind users to the platform, forcing both users and service providers to absorb these added costs. Moreover, platforms invest heavily in their ecosystems, incorporating a broader range of participants and evolving bilateral connections into multilateral interactions. Once established, these mature ecosystems exhibit high stability and even self-sustaining growth, making them difficult to disrupt.

In the digital economy, platforms, as rule-setters, naturally occupy the apex of the ecosystem, wielding significant value leverage. However, this is detrimental to overall societal welfare. Monopolistic platforms tend to suppress potential competitors, using existing rules or capital acquisitions to maintain their status, deviating from their original intent to reduce information asymmetry through openness and connectivity. Practices like forced exclusivity, where platforms use non-economic forces to eliminate competitors and maintain market exclusivity, are common. For instance, ByteDance has prevented users from sharing videos directly to Tencent's social media app, WeChat, or Alibaba's e-commerce platform, Taobao, blocking payments via WeChat Pay.

Monopolistic platforms also stifle innovation. Their core role should be to reduce information asymmetry, thereby serving societal and economic efficiency. However, distorting information through monopolies exacerbates asymmetry. Once a monopoly is established, platforms tend to maintain it, often resorting to price manipulation, discriminatory pricing, collusion, or illegal mergers, all of which suppress innovation and competition.

Worse yet, platform monopolies lead to the abuse of "digital power," a growing intolerance for Web 2.0. Data, a powerful control element, is owned by digital platforms. Though people appear free in the digital world, they are deeply controlled by platforms. This control permeates our digital existence—we are tracked, analyzed, labeled, targeted by e-commerce and advertising, recommended news and music, categorized, scored, censored, or even manipulated.

For example, platforms can precisely understand users' interests, preferences, and behaviors through data analysis and algorithms, enabling targeted positioning, recommendations, and marketing. The concept of "echo chambers" is a result of such targeted content, where users are increasingly exposed to information that aligns with their existing beliefs, reducing exposure to differing views and fostering a homogenized discourse.

In the Web 2.0 era, the evolution of big data and AI has led to personalized, isolated information silos. Whether through active selection like Jike's circle or passive customization like algorithmic feeds on TikTok or Toutiao, these designs ostensibly create quality discussion spaces within niches. However, they also isolate users from content that might challenge their views, confining their information access to familiar comfort zones.

Users become entrenched in echo chambers, interacting with familiar content and viewpoints, their tastes and opinions constrained by algorithms. They avoid seeking out conflicting information, indulging in endless scrolling without the need for discussion or challenge. Platforms prioritize their interests over media responsibilities, focusing on commercial gains rather than balanced information dissemination.

This personalized service may seem to enhance user experience, but in reality, it strengthens digital platforms' control and influence, exacerbating digital power imbalances and abuses. Such examples are pervasive, touching nearly every aspect of our digital lives, illustrating how the digital power of tech giants extends beyond the economy into politics and culture, growing increasingly dominant.

6.1.3 Restoring Data Sovereignty to Users

In the Web 2.0 era, the cornerstone of the platform economy was the collection and control of extensive user data by centralized entities. The rise of Web 3.0, however, challenges this foundational aspect. Unlike its predecessor, Web 3.0 is characterized by the empowerment of users through sovereign digital identities, signaling a shift of data control back to users and potentially dismantling the monopolies of Internet platforms established in the Web 2.0 era. In this new era, individuals will possess control over their identities and data, representing a significant technological advancement and a reimagining of freedom, rights, and value.

In the future, personal data will emerge as one of our most significant assets. Enhanced by AI, individuals will unlock profound insights from their data, deriving valuable information. Quantum computing will facilitate decentralized processing, enabling seamless data interactions, while quantum communication will safeguard personal data from unauthorized exploitation. DNA storage offers an expansive repository for personal data, ensuring its preservation and reliability.

This environment empowers everyone to be both creators and consumers within the digital landscape. AI will simplify the production of high-quality digital content while quantum computing and communication expand market access and opportunities, ensuring the swift and secure distribution of creative output. Moreover, individuals will freely engage with others' content, fostering a direct connection between creators and consumers that encourages diversity and innovation.

Digital identity becomes the bedrock for economic engagement, encapsulating more than just basic information but also encompassing skills, interests, and social networks. Enhanced by AI, these digital identities will strengthen social interactions. Individuals can utilize these identities to design personal business models, issue digital currencies, and generate income, cultivating a decentralized economy that bestows greater autonomy and freedom, enabling broad participation in value creation and sharing.

When Web 3.0 fully materializes, we will evolve from mere "users" to active participants in the economy—be it as creators, consumers, or even platforms themselves. Similar to how today's Internet influencers develop business models around their audience, in the Web 3.0 era, everyone can use a decentralized network to establish their business models, marking a shift to a more diverse, freely centered digital era of human rights.

These transformations will extend beyond the economic domain, influencing social interactions, education, entertainment, and more, profoundly affecting societal operations. Without a doubt, Web 3.0 will redefine power, value, and participation, heralding a new era for every individual.

6.2 Data Trading: The Business Core of Web 3.0

The evolution of digital society into Web 3.0 is not merely a technological upgrade or a new iteration of the Internet; it signifies a fundamental shift in the paradigms of online communication and transaction.

In the current Web 2.0 phase, our data, communications, and transactions are largely at the mercy of centralized platforms, such as social media corporations and e-commerce giants. These entities dictate the flow of data and reap the benefits. However, Web 3.0 turns this model on its head. In this emerging paradigm, every individual owns their digital identity and data, holding sole control over it. Consequently, transactions based on personal data form the crux of Web 3.0's commercial landscape.

6.2.1 Exploring Data Trading

Today, data has ascended as a critical production element and strategic asset in human society, surpassing even oil in its financial value, especially as we edge closer to the AI era. The capacity to gather, analyze, and utilize data has swiftly become a pivotal focus of international competition. As

Web 3.0 unfolds, paralleled by deeper digital integration in society, the significance of data resources is set to amplify.

However, unlocking the full potential of data necessitates open access and circulation. Various nations have already initiated explorations into data trading, recognizing its vital role in the future digital economy.

The United States epitomizes a fully market-driven approach to data trading. Its advanced information industry provides a solid supply and demand dynamic, laying the groundwork for the formation and development of a data trading and circulation market. In the process of building this market, the US has established policies and regulations to encourage the growth of the data trading industry, further standardizing its evolution.

One key initiative is the establishment of an open government data mechanism. Following the release of the Open Government Directive in 2009, the US government accelerated the data opening process through Data.gov, a "one-stop" government data service platform. Here, data from federal and state governments, departments, and civil organizations is consolidated, offering public access to diverse data sets from economics to healthcare. This platform not only disseminates data but also allows developers to process and redevelop it.

In contrast, the European Union aims to promote data circulation through policy and legal measures, striving to unify its member states into a single digital market. The General Data Protection Regulation (GDPR), effective since May 2018, exemplifies this effort, emphasizing the balance between data protection rights and free data flow. Despite its strict regulations, which initially impacted venture capital investments in EU tech firms, GDPR has set a benchmark for data legislation globally.

Germany offers a "practice-first" approach, building secure data exchange paths within industries to foster interconnectedness and a robust data-sharing ecosystem. The UK's open banking strategy, which allows secure data sharing through APIs in the financial sector, demonstrates another innovative approach to harnessing data's value.

Japan's creation of a "data bank" model reflects a tailored approach to maximizing personal data's value, showcasing a bridge between individuals and the data trading market. This model emphasizes contract-based management and utilization of personal data, contributing to the vitality of the data trading market.

In China, significant strides have been made in data sharing through the national data-sharing platform, integrating data from various government levels and departments. This platform supports numerous administrative and business processes, showcasing the government's commitment to data openness.

While these developments mark significant progress, the majority of data trading still primarily involves enterprises, with individuals facing substantial barriers to entry. This is largely due to the monopolistic nature of large tech companies, legal and privacy concerns, and the need for technical knowledge and resources. However, the advent of Web 3.0 promises a new era where individuals can actively participate in data trading, leveraging their data sovereignty to engage in transactions on their terms. This shift will democratize data trading, enabling individuals to monetize their data while contributing to a more dynamic and equitable digital economy.

6.2.2 Building Data Exchanges

In the journey toward open, fluid, and transactional data, data exchanges play a pivotal role. Their necessity and significance stem from addressing chronic issues in data trading.

In the Web 2.0 era, propelled by rapid advancements in cloud computing and the Internet of Things (IoT), the digitization and intelligentization of humans and objects have become a reality. This trend has not only fostered the widespread application of big data but also unveiled substantial market potential, giving rise to new business models and a comprehensive ecosystem around the value chain of big data. Consequently, the societal recognition of data's value has soared, making data-driven decision-making integral for both governments and corporations. Alongside this, the demand for data sharing and openness has intensified.

However, this leads to complications. Despite breakthroughs in data storage and mining, "data silos" remain prevalent due to various stakeholders' interest-driven reluctance to share data. This issue is especially pronounced in democratic countries where substantial tension exists between individual privacy and the commercialization of big data. The fragmented nature of data ownership, alongside the absence of individual data sovereignty, significantly hinders commercialization efforts.

While data circulation isn't new, the absence of comprehensive legal frameworks related to data trading across different legal systems impedes the market. The lack of trading regulations, uncertain pricing standards, and information asymmetry between parties contribute to high transaction costs and uncertainty regarding data quality, severely limiting data asset liquidity.

These challenges have allowed Internet giants, governments, and large corporations to amass significant data resources, granting them considerable influence and control in the data domain. These entities have become data oligarchs, dominating the data market and negatively impacting free market competition and consumer rights protection.

Additionally, the information economy naturally grapples with the "Arrow paradox," which highlights the unique nature of information (or data) compared to conventional goods. The value of information is difficult to ascertain upfront for buyers, as its worth becomes evident only after the acquisition, and it can be replicated and distributed, eliminating the need for further purchases.

The value of data is context-dependent and varies based on application and processing methods. Different enterprises may value the same data differently, and the market value of data can fluctuate based on how it's processed and analyzed. As a result, buyers struggle to assess data quality and value accurately, potentially leading to overpayments for underwhelming outcomes. Conversely, sellers might undervalue their data due to a lack of understanding of buyer needs or concerns about data security and misuse.

The current state of data trading is akin to an invisible barrier between data-rich suppliers and eager demanders, where information asymmetry and communication barriers hinder data's commercial potential. This inefficient resource allocation necessitates a transparent, regulated trading platform to unravel the complexities of data transactions.

This is where data exchanges become crucial. They serve not just as marketplaces but as vital connectors between data supply and demand, engines driving data flow and creating new value. Imagine a platform where suppliers and demanders can communicate more directly and efficiently and where information is unveiled, fostering closer collaboration and innovation in the data landscape.

Currently, there have been numerous global endeavors to establish data exchanges. Since their inception around 2008, there have been comprehensive data trading centers like BDEX, Infochimps, Mashape, and RapidAPI in the United States, as well as many that focus on niche sectors. These include Factual in the location data sphere, Quandl and Qlik Data Market in economic and financial data, GE Predix and the Fraunhofer Society's Industrial Data Space project in industrial data, and DataCoup and Personal in personal data trading.

Beyond specialized platforms, leading IT companies worldwide, leveraging their extensive cloud services and data resources, are also building their data trading platforms. This move aims to create a core mechanism for fostering data circulation ecosystems. Examples include Amazon AWS Data Exchange, Google Cloud, Microsoft Azure Marketplace, LinkedIn's Fliptop platform, Twitter's Gnip platform, Fujitsu's Data Plaza, and Oracle Data Cloud. Currently, these international data trading entities adopt a fully market-driven model, with data products mainly focusing on consumer behavior, location dynamics, business financial information, population health data, and insurance claim records.

China's data exchange journey began in 2015, a pivotal year for its development. In April 2015, the Guiyang Big Data Exchange was launched under the support of the Guiyang State-Owned Assets Supervision and Administration Commission and executed its first transaction. In August, the first data exchange in the central China region, the Yangtze River Big Data Exchange, was established in Wuhan. By the end of 2021, nearly a hundred various data trading platforms were operational in China, including notable ones like the Beijing International Big Data Exchange, Shanghai Big Data Exchange, East China Jiangsu Big Data Exchange, Central Plains Big Data Exchange, and U-Data.

Besides professional data exchanges, leading Chinese IT companies have also been developing their data trading platforms, such as Alibaba Cloud, Tencent Cloud, and Baidu Cloud, each with its API market, along with JD Wanxiang and Inspur Tianyuan, among others. Juhe Data, an API technology service company, has accumulated over 500 categories of API interfaces, with daily calls reaching 300 million and over 1.2 million cooperating clients across fields like intelligent manufacturing, AI, and 5G applications. In 2021, with strong national policy support, regions like Shenzhen, Shanghai, and Guizhou, capitalizing on their unique characteristics, introduced local "data regulations" and established data exchanges, fostering a new model of localized data development and governance, promoting the resource and asset transformation of local data.

6.2.3 Infrastructure in the Web 3.0 Era

It's worth noting that the data exchanges of the Web 2.0 era are still in their nascent stages. Even though leading data exchanges have reached transaction volumes in the hundreds of millions, many data exchanges haven't become as active as anticipated and are still in the exploratory phase. There are five primary reasons for this.

First is the issue of commercial boundaries of data, which involves the balance between data security and openness, as well as privacy and commercialization. During big data transactions, it's crucial to define the scope of data usage—determining what data falls under confidential national security and what can be used in the open commercial domain, alongside setting commercial boundary standards for data.

Second is the issue of data classification standards—defining categories for various data types and how to classify them. Given the diverse nature of big data, systematic categorization is essential for better transaction and utilization.

Third is data pricing, a complex challenge that arises after data classification. Various factors, including data scarcity, quality, accuracy, timeliness, market demand, and competitive conditions, need to be considered to reflect the data's commercial value accurately.

Fourth is the data trading mechanism and profit distribution. The current data market can be segmented into government governance data, industrial data, financial data, public service data, and personal commercial application data. The first four segments have relatively straightforward trading and benefit-sharing mechanisms. In contrast, personal, commercial application data, inherently generated by individual users, presents significant focus and challenges in data trading.

Fifth is the necessity of data legislation. Both personal data privacy and commercial aspects require specific laws to define, safeguard boundaries and rights, ensuring clear and precise legal rules for commercial activities to prevent misuse and disruptions in normal life.

The advent of the Web 3.0 era, emphasizing individual data sovereignty and digital identity rights, promises solutions to these issues. For instance, addressing commercial boundary issues will rely on establishing data ownership and personal data control rights. Individuals will have full authority over their data, including what can be used commercially and under what conditions it can be shared. Personalized data classification standards will cater to diverse and specific needs, allowing individuals to manage and protect their data better while offering more flexible trading options.

In the future, data pricing will increasingly be determined by individual data owners. They will set prices based on data's value, scarcity, and market demand, facilitating open trading on data exchanges. This market-driven pricing mechanism will better reflect the data's true value, promoting fair and efficient transactions.

With personalized data sovereignty, we can expect a fair and transparent data trading mechanism and profit distribution model. Individuals will directly participate in data trading, choosing how and under what conditions their data is exchanged while benefiting from the profits. Data exchanges will provide technical support and legal safeguards to ensure secure and compliant transactions, protecting individual data rights.

In essence, data trading represents the commercial core of the Web 3.0 era, with data exchanges serving as foundational infrastructure. Through these exchanges, data from various domains can be traded and collaborated across boundaries, fostering integration and innovation. This not only supplies rich data resources for emerging technologies like AI but also signifies the openness, circulation, and value realization of data resources, driving the data economy and providing new momentum and opportunities for digital transformation in human society.

6.3 Producing Valuable Data

Labor creates value, an age-old adage central to Marx's theory of labor value.

Labor is the foundation of human society's emergence and development, pivotal to the continuation of world history and the perpetual evolution of human civilization. However, in today's era, marked by rapid technological advancements and continuous growth in productivity, the tools employed for labor are increasingly advanced, from machines replacing physical labor to AI supplanting intellectual labor, reducing the human labor required.

With the maturity of technologies like AI, quantum computing, and quantum communication, coupled with the onset of Web 3.0, humanity is poised to step fully into a digital world. Here, all industrial and agricultural production tasks could be undertaken by robots and automated factories. This leads to a pressing question: when labor becomes redundant, what can replace "labor" to create value?

6.3.1 From Industrial to Data Labor

The rapid advancement of groundbreaking technologies, notably AI, quantum computing, and data science, heralds a significant transition in the industrial landscape. As we progress into the Web 3.0 era, the notion of labor and production is being fundamentally redefined.

Historically, the first and second industrial revolutions introduced automation, significantly enhancing productivity and extending human capabilities in manufacturing. The advent of the assembly line and standardized production epitomized this era, setting the stage for more sophisticated automation technologies. The third industrial revolution, marked by the integration of computing and information technology, furthered automation, introducing systems with minimal or no human intervention in production processes. The establishment of the world's first experimental "unmanned factory" in 1984 in Tsukuba Science City, Japan, symbolized a leap toward full automation in manufacturing.

Four decades later, the integration of AI into production processes exemplifies a new paradigm—where "unmanned" operations are not just feasible but increasingly common. This shift is not confined to physical labor; AI is progressively assuming roles traditionally associated with intellectual labor. For instance, ChatGPT, with its sophisticated capabilities in coding, creative writing, and conversational interactions, exemplifies AGI's potential to undertake complex intellectual tasks, challenging the notion of human exclusivity in intellectual endeavors.

As we contemplate a future where AI and automation pervade all facets of production and intellectual labor, a fundamental question emerges: what will be the source of value in a landscape where human labor is no longer central? Drawing from Marx's labor theory of value, which posits that labor is the source of all value, the evolving landscape prompts a reevaluation of this theory in the context of digital and automated production.

The digital era introduces a new dimension to labor and value creation. Digital labor, characterized by the generation and processing of data, becomes a pivotal aspect of value creation. In this new context, data is not just an asset but a form of labor product, transformed into valuable commodities through algorithmic processing and computational analysis.

In the Web 3.0 era, where data sovereignty and digital identity are emphasized, individuals contribute to value creation through their digital interactions and behaviors. This shift signifies a transition from traditional forms of labor to digital labor, where the creation, exchange, and utilization of data underpin economic and social structures.

As data becomes a key factor of production alongside traditional resources, its role in generating value is increasingly recognized. The transformation of raw data into actionable insights and knowledge through computational processes echoes the industrial transformation of raw materials into goods. This process, facilitated by advanced algorithms and computational power, underscores the evolving nature of labor and value in the digital age.

In summary, the Web 3.0 era redefines the concept of labor and value creation, positioning data and digital interactions at the heart of economic and social dynamics. As we navigate this new era, the understanding and utilization of data will be central to our collective economic and social advancement, marking a paradigm shift in how value is perceived and generated in our interconnected digital world.

6.3.2 Enhancing Personal Data Value

Web 3.0 marks a significant shift toward data sovereignty, where individuals regain control over their personal data. In this new era, the focus shifts to how we can produce more valuable data, effectively package it, and trade it on data exchanges. This is crucial since, in Web 3.0, data trading becomes a central business activity, with personal data's value directly impacting individual assets.

To generate valuable data in Web 3.0, we need to adopt a fresh mindset. Unlike Web 2.0, where personal data was often viewed as incidental snippets of information, Web 3.0 encourages us to recognize and actively manage our data's potential value. This means being proactive in capturing and understanding data from our daily behaviors, health, and social interactions, acknowledging its worth not only to ourselves but to others.

Behavioral data, for instance, is immensely valuable. The data we generate through our daily activities, like online engagement and social interactions, becomes a crucial output. Such data has applications in areas like personalized recommendations, targeted marketing, and healthcare management. With advancements in healthcare technology, personal health data will also play a pivotal role, offering insights for personalized healthcare and wellness management.

Looking ahead, the metaverse presents a novel avenue for data generation, offering a plethora of behavioral insights through virtual interactions and activities. Data from these interactions can be packaged as commodities for trade-in data marketplaces.

Equally important is data quality and integrity. In Web 3.0, the quality of data significantly influences its value. Ensuring data is authentic, accurate, and timely is essential to avoid misinformation. High-quality data collection methods and regular updates are crucial to maintain data integrity.

Beyond data generation, processing, and packaging data are key to enhancing its value, presenting new opportunities in Web 3.0. Future training programs could equip individuals to commercialize their data effectively, similar to current e-commerce or media training programs but focused on personal data optimization.

This training could cover a range of skills, from employing AI assistants in data management to categorizing and analyzing everyday data. In the Web 3.0 era, utilizing AI technology to process and analyze personal data can reveal hidden value, and support personal, commercial, and new economic potentials in the digital economy.

By engaging in personal data commercialization training, individuals can gain the skills needed to elevate the business value of their data, enhancing their understanding and uncovering commercial opportunities within their data sets. This not only supports individual economic independence but also fosters the growth and dynamism of the digital economy.

—CHAPTER 7—

Navigating the Path to Web 3.0

7.1 Technical Milestones for Web 3.0's Emergence

Web 3.0 envisions a future where digital identity and personal data sovereignty are central. In this envisioned future, every individual has the opportunity to participate actively and exercise their rights, transitioning from mere users of social networks to being in control of their digital presence. Each interaction, be it a click, a message, or any online activity, contributes new value to the network, integrating every user into the economic fabric.

However, while this vision is inspiring, its realization requires grounding in current technological advancements. The fulfillment of Web 3.0's promise depends on the development and maturation of pioneering technologies such as AI, quantum computing, quantum communication, and DNA storage. These technologies, essential to the Web 3.0 infrastructure, are still evolving and have yet to reach their full potential.

7.1.1 Limitations of Quantum Technology

Quantum technology is indispensable in the Web 3.0 era, especially quantum computing and communication, which are crucial for truly decentralized computation and ultra-secure communication in Web 3.0. Yet, quantum technology is still in the developmental phase and not yet practical.

- **THE LONG ROAD TO QUANTUM COMPUTING COMMERCIALIZATION**

Quantum computing is a foundational technology for the future digital world, vital not just for decentralized computing in Web 3.0 but also for the next breakthroughs in AI.

Despite the surge in AI, exemplified by ChatGPT, which is raising hopes for AGI, this also escalates the demand for computational power. However, due to physical constraints, there's a limit to how much computational power can increase. In 1965, Intel co-founder Gordon Moore predicted that the number of components on an integrated circuit would double approximately every 18 to 24 months. Moore's Law has been a profound indicator of IT progress globally. However, classical computers will eventually hit physical limits, continuing Moore's Law with silicon transistors as their basic component.

As transistors in computers shrink, the barriers between them thin out. At 3 nanometers, only a dozen atoms might form the barrier. At such microscopic levels, electrons can exhibit quantum tunneling, making it challenging to represent "0" and "1" accurately—this is the so-called "Moore's Law ceiling." While there are suggestions to change materials to enhance the internal barrier of transistors, the reality is that no material can prevent electron tunneling. Moreover, increasing data centers to compensate for classical computational power is impractical due to sustainability and energy reduction needs. Thus, quantum computing emerges as a significant breakthrough for enhancing computational power.

However, the commercialization of quantum computing remains exploratory. Despite some major breakthroughs at theoretical and experimental levels, including achievements in the United States, Europe, and China, with some beginning commercial applications, these applications are still in their infancy or experimental stages.

The creation of quantum computers hinges on mastering superposition and entanglement: without superposition, qubits would merely mimic classical bits, unable to concurrently process multiple computations. Absent entanglement, even if qubits are superposed, they can't unlock additional computational insights due to their independent states.

The commercial value of qubits lies in effectively harnessing super-position and entanglement, or "quantum coherence," where qubits' inter-linked states allow one qubit's alteration to influence the rest. Quantum computation demands maintaining this coherence across all qubits, but interaction with external environments leads to rapid coherence loss, known as "decoherence."

Quantum algorithms aim to minimize quantum gate usage, completing computations before decoherence and errors intervene. This often involves a hybrid approach, delegating extensive computational tasks to classical computers. A functional quantum computer is estimated to require 1,000 to 100,000 qubits.

Skeptics like Mikhail Dyakonov caution that the vast array of continuous parameters needed to define a quantum computer's state—on the order of 2^{1000} or around 10^{300}—could be its downfall. Managing these parameters is daunting, with their quantity surpassing the universe's subatomic particles. Ineffectively controlling these parameters could compromise quantum computers, posing a significant risk.

The threshold theorem suggests overcoming this by ensuring each quantum bit's error rate in gates stays below a certain threshold, enabling indefinite quantum computing at the cost of increased qubit numbers. Extra qubits would serve error correction, akin to telecommunication systems' error-checking bits, but this escalates the number of physical qubits necessary, reaching astronomical figures.

Contrasting with classical computers, where robust noise resistance allows accurate operation despite voltage fluctuations, quantum bits' extreme sensitivity to noise stems from their minuscule energy differential between states. This sensitivity underscores why quantum error correction remains a formidable challenge, potentially imposing significant computational burdens and hindering quantum computer development.

Commercially, the quantum tech sector has yet to see cumulative profits, with immense R&D investments and ongoing product trials. Industry observer Doug Finke predicts most quantum startups won't survive the next decade in their current form. While there may be some winners, many will likely close, merge, or acquire. The lack of a unified technological direction and commercial standard further complicates the path to quantum computing commercialization.

Despite breakthroughs and global investment in quantum computing, bridging the gap to widespread commercial use requires navigating substantial obstacles. The journey from theoretical to practical quantum computing entails transforming the elusive and unstable nature of quantum entanglement into a manageable "stability" technology, a crucial step for the technology's future.

- **CHALLENGES OF QUANTUM COMMUNICATION**

The essence of quantum communication lies in utilizing quantum entanglement for information transfer, which encompasses quantum key distribution (QKD) and QT.

QKD allows secure key-sharing between sender and receiver, leveraging one-time pad encryption for secure communication. It utilizes the unpredictability and non-clonability of quantum mechanics to ensure undetectable information transfer. This requires establishing a secure key-sharing channel that eavesdroppers cannot access, followed by integrating this with conventional security communication technology for encryption and decryption of classical information. QT, on the other hand, is about transferring quantum state information directly based on distributed quantum entangled states and quantum joint measurements without physically moving the information carrier.

However, both QKD and QT face unresolved technical challenges. For QKD, the issue is the theoretical and experimental work hasn't yet surpassed the rate-distance limit for QKD without relays. This means our current methods of transmitting quantum keys haven't exceeded the constraints of classical physics. Distance becomes a limiting factor in no-relay situations, as quantum states degrade during transmission due to signal attenuation. Increasing distance reduces photon count, impacting the key distribution rate. This can be partially mitigated by boosting photon emission rates and using efficient detectors, but challenges remain for long-distance transmission.

Noise in measurement devices is another constraint. Even in ideal conditions, measurement devices introduce some level of noise. As distance increases, signal attenuation reduces the received photon count, increasing the relative noise ratio. When noise exceeds a certain threshold, key distribution becomes impractical, limiting QKD systems' effectiveness in long-distance communication due to reduced signal strength and relative noise increase.

QT remains an experimental phenomenon. For instance, in 2008, scientists at the University of Tokyo teleported quantum information across several kilometers within the city. By integrating QT with optical fibers, the team could send entangled photons over long distances. In 2011, the first successful hundred-kilometer-level free-space QT and entanglement distribution were achieved internationally, addressing long-distance information transmission for communication satellites. In 2015, NIST researchers transmitted quantum information through 100 km of optical fiber, quadrupling the previous distance. In 2019, Nanjing University initiated experiments on air-ground quantum entanglement distribution and measurement using drones, which carried optical transmitters to complete quantum entanglement distribution measurement with a ground receiving station over 200 m. Yet, these breakthroughs remain experimental rather than practical, indicating QT is still some distance away from everyday application.

7.1.2 Tackling the Cost Challenges of DNA Storage

DNA storage, a futuristic storage solution, began research in the 2000s. Early experiments included encoding Einstein's famous equation "$E = mc^2$" into bacterial DNA in 2000 and a Disney song segment in 2003. By 2010, scientists had embedded the names of project scientists into the DNA of the first synthetic cell.

This technology demonstrated the potential to store virtually anything in DNA, from textual documents to film data. However, the process traditionally required significant human intervention until breakthroughs by Microsoft and the University of Washington. Their research introduced random access in DNA storage, allowing for the retrieval of specific data segments without needing to read entire sequences—a significant step forward.

Yet, the challenges of synthesis speed and cost remain. Current synthesis rates are in kilobytes per second, while established cloud storage systems achieve gigabytes per second. To be competitive, DNA writing speed needs to increase by six orders of magnitude.

To boost data processing, scientists are exploring parallel DNA synthesis, akin to parallel computing. In 2021, Microsoft developed a nanoscale DNA storage device capable of synthesizing 2,650 base sequences simultaneously per square centimeter, significantly increasing throughput.

Increased throughput means lower costs. Currently, DNA storage costs stand at $800 million per terabyte, starkly higher than the $16 per terabyte for tape storage. Despite seeming non-competitive, DNA storage's high density, small volume, and long-term stability offer significant advantages over traditional data centers, which incur high maintenance and regular hardware updates.

The cost of DNA storage has dramatically decreased compared to the past, mirroring the reduction in genome sequencing costs—from $2.7 billion over 15 years for the first human genome to $1,000 for a sequence today. Given the exponential growth of technology, commercial DNA storage could soon be a reality.

As these cutting-edge technologies mature, Web 3.0 will move closer from concept to reality, marking a significant stride toward a digital future.

7.1.3 Energy Consumption in Web 3.0

As we edge closer to a digitized world, the upcoming Web 3.0 era will unavoidably confront the issue of energy consumption. Presently, AI alone guzzles substantial amounts of energy. The essence of computation involves transforming data from disorder to order, necessitating a significant energy input. A 2023 report by the *Economist* highlights that high-performance computing facilities, including supercomputers, are becoming major energy consumers. The International Energy Agency estimates that data centers account for 1.5% to 2% of global electricity usage, approximately equal to the entire UK's consumption, which is predicted to rise to 4% by 2030.

The energy used, if not sourced from renewables, leads to carbon emissions. Training AI models like GPT-3 is energy-intensive, consuming 1,287 MWh of electricity, equivalent to 552 tons of carbon emissions. Sustainable data researcher Kaspar Ludvigsen notes the difficulty in accurately measuring carbon output due to the lack of standardized methods and the additional power required by reinforcement learning, suggesting that the actual emissions from training ChatGPT might exceed the estimated figures.

In the operational phase, the power consumption of using ChatGPT, while minimal per interaction, could accumulate significantly given the billions of daily global interactions, potentially making it a substantial source of carbon emissions.

AI's energy consumption extends beyond electricity to water usage. Google's 2023 environmental report revealed that its data centers alone consumed over 5.2 billion gallons of water in 2022, up 20% from the previous year. Data centers, the backbone of the digital world, require immense energy to function, especially for cooling systems.

While alternative energy sources like ocean thermal energy and natural mechanical energies (wind, tidal, etc.) are seen as hopeful, solar energy stands out as the most viable long-term solution. The sun's nuclear fusion process emits vast amounts of heat and light, nourishing the earth for billions of years.

Photosynthesis, the process by which microorganisms and plants convert sunlight into organic carbon, setting a precedent for energy manipulation, is a fundamental life-sustaining technology on the earth. Considering renewables and reserves, solar energy is the only source capable of meeting humanity's long-term energy needs, vastly surpassing hydropower, wind energy, and other alternatives.

Nuclear fusion, generating power without nuclear waste or carbon emissions, is gaining attention as a key to resolving global carbon issues. In 2023, Microsoft partnered with fusion startup Helion Energy, planning to purchase power from the world's first fusion power plant by 2028.

Both past and future energy revolutions are deeply intertwined with scientific advancements. Discoveries in natural phenomena lead to new energy technologies, driving profound changes across society and technology.

The intrinsic logic of energy revolutions reflects the evolving demands of human civilization—from survival in primitive societies to enhanced quality of life and industrial production in feudal societies to the accelerated demand for transportation, information, and entertainment during the Industrial Revolution. The forthcoming Web 3.0 era will witness unprecedented energy demands, propelling us into a new chapter of energy development and consumption.

7.2 Challenges to the Realization of Web 3.0

We've acknowledged that at the heart of Web 3.0 lies the "restructuring of Internet control," empowering users to manage their digital identities and personal data independently rather than depending on centralized entities for services. Realizing Web 3.0's vision faces numerous challenges beyond just technical hurdles; it also confronts opposition from centralized giants and regulatory obstacles. Additionally, awakening user awareness is indispensable.

7.2.1 Demystifying Web 3.0

By 2021, Web 3.0 was dubbed the tech buzzword of the year by Reuters, with many tech companies and pioneers voicing their commitment to embracing Web 3.0. Yet, three years on, Web 3.0 remains an ambiguous and broad concept. While many are aware of Web 3.0, its exact nature remains elusive.

Reuters defines Web 3.0 as the next phase of the Internet: a "decentralized" Internet based on blockchain technology. In this model, users own the platforms and applications, a stark contrast to the current Internet landscape.

Ethereum appears closest to this definition, with its vast array of dApps, including Uniswap and Compound, allowing users to engage without registration or authentication, thus protecting privacy and enhancing control over personal identity and data usage. However, Ethereum's applications predominantly reside in the financial sector, with limited broader reach, and not all are as decentralized as they claim, as evidenced by frequent incidents of project insiders compromising their own platforms.

Elon Musk has been dismissive of Web 3.0, even labeling it as "nonsense" in 2021 and questioning its reality versus its portrayal as a marketing buzzword. Musk's conservative stance contrasts with his usual embrace of future technologies, suggesting he views the current phase of Web 3.0 as more hype than substance.

The confusion surrounding Web 3.0 stems from a lack of consensus on its definition, with varying interpretations among organizations, institutions, and individuals. This has been compounded by market hype that lacks substantial implementation, leaving Web 3.0 as a niche, high-barrier industry, often skewed toward speculative digital currency ventures.

Despite this, a consensus on Web 3.0 is forming, with increasing discussions and breakthroughs in frontier technologies clarifying its vision. At its core, Web 3.0 aims to restructure Internet control, giving users independence from centralized service providers and more authority over their identities and data, eventually redistributing commercial value previously monopolized by Internet giants.

Before this vision materializes, clearer definitions and heightened user awareness of reclaiming control are necessary. In the Web 2.0 era, users became accustomed to entrusting their data and identity to centralized platforms in exchange for convenience. This model led to data misuse and centralized commercial value, diminishing individual rights. In the Web 3.0 era, fostering a sense of digital identity and data sovereignty is crucial, recognizing every individual's right to manage and utilize their digital presence and personal data. Only with a shift toward autonomy, privacy, and security can Web 3.0's realization and progression be truly catalyzed.

7.2.2 The Resistance of Centralized Giants

The vision of Web 3.0 is undoubtedly promising, portraying a future where every user becomes a creator in the Internet ecosystem rather than being merely a tool for platforms to generate traffic and earn advertising revenue. Web 3.0 harbors the significant characteristic of "eliminating authority" on the Internet, with some even arguing that it represents a comprehensive victory of the public against the giants. However, achieving this victory is no easy feat, especially given the obstacles, particularly those from centralized giants.

In fact, tech giants from the Web 2.0 era have also made forays into Web 3.0. Internationally, Google has overtly displayed its enthusiasm and determination for Web 3.0. In May 2022, Google Cloud Vice President Amit Zavery informed employees via email about the immense potential of the Web 3.0 market, noting many clients' requests for increased support for Web 3.0 and cryptocurrency-related technologies. Consequently, within its $3 billion headquarters, Google officially established its first Web 3.0 department, aiming to provide backend services for blockchain developers and focus on the infrastructure of the Web 3.0 world.

Google Cloud is likened to the Web 3.0 wave to the rise of open-source and the Internet 10–15 years ago, stating on its official blog that blockchain and digital assets are transforming how the world stores and transfers information and value.

In the cloud service provider sphere, Google isn't the first Internet giant to venture into Web 3.0—Amazon's AWS and Microsoft's Azure had already made earlier moves. In the realm of social media, Twitter and Meta have engaged in fierce competition. Jack Dorsey advocate for Web 3.0, introduced several measures favorable to Web 3.0 and cryptocurrencies during his last two years at Twitter, including Twitter Space and NFT functionalities on the platform. However, despite these efforts, Dorsey ultimately had to leave Twitter due to profitability concerns.

Meta, lagging behind competitors, accelerated its exploration of NFTs and Web 3.0. On June 30, 2022, a Meta spokesperson announced on Twitter that the company had begun testing NFTs on Facebook for select US creators, with plans to expand support to Solana and Flow NFTs.

E-commerce giants like eBay and Shopify have also delved into the NFT and Web 3.0 market, with eBay allowing NFT transactions on its platform and acquiring NFT trading platform KnowsOrigin in June 2022. Shopify introduced a service for selling NFT goods, enabling sellers to create and sell NFT products.

In China, major Internet companies such as Tencent, ByteDance, Baidu, JD.com, Bilibili, and Xiaohongshu have rushed into the NFT industry. TikTok, Douyin's overseas version, placed NFTs on Immutable X in 2021, and Tencent's investment in Australian NFT gaming company Immutable resulted in a $200 million funding round.

However, it's crucial to acknowledge that the so-called Web 3.0 projects and ventures based on blockchain and NFTs are not genuinely Web 3.0. Internet giants are entering the Web 3.0 industry mainly to position themselves for the next Internet era, aiming to gain an early advantage. True Web 3.0 will disrupt Web 2.0, shatter the platform economy of the Web 2.0 era, and reshape the business model centered around data trading. Transitioning from Web 2.0 to 3.0, from centralization to decentralization, and from platform sovereignty to user sovereignty will undoubtedly encounter resistance from today's Internet giants.

Centralized giants possess immense resources and influence, having accumulated vast user bases, data assets, and market shares over the past decades, forming near-monopolistic positions. They wield significant capital, cutting-edge technology, and extensive user data, easily hindering competitors' growth and reinforcing their dominance through acquisitions and mergers. Breaking this monopoly requires robust antitrust laws and policies, as well as fair competition regulatory mechanisms.

Moreover, centralized giants hold considerable advantages in technology, services, and market presence. They can continuously introduce new products and services to meet user demands and capture market share while using their dominant positions to restrict competitors, such as through blocking, filtering, or discriminatory algorithms. Therefore, achieving Web 3.0's vision necessitates an open, fair, and transparent market environment that encourages innovation and competition, protecting the rights of small businesses and entrepreneurs.

Additionally, centralized giants control vast amounts of user data, granting them significant informational advantages. They can use data analytics and algorithm optimization for personalized recommendations, precise marketing, and user behavior manipulation, further solidifying their market position and profit sources.

Moreover, centralized giants possess vast user data, granting them significant informational advantages. They utilize data analysis and algorithm optimization to deliver personalized recommendations, targeted marketing, and user behavior manipulation, thereby reinforcing their market dominance and profit sources.

An additional consideration for Web 3.0's realization is identifying who will provide substantial incentives during the early stages of a project when commercial value shifts to the users. A prime example is the intense competition between Didi and Uber in the ride-hailing market, which ultimately transformed how people commute. Without centralized entities driving innovation, the growth pace of Web 3.0 applications might slow down, and their iteration efficiency could significantly trail behind that of centralized giants.

However, the outlook isn't entirely grim. Historically, new technological shifts have often paved the way for the emergence of new industry giants. For instance, in the transition from Web 1.0 to 2.0, amid Google's dominance, social media behemoths like Facebook and Twitter were born. Similarly, in China, despite Alibaba and Tencent's stronghold, disruptors like ByteDance have emerged. Large corporations from each era, burdened by their size, often struggle with comprehensive strategic shifts, lacking the nimbleness of new challengers.

7.2.3 Navigating the Complexities of Government Regulation

In discussing the development hurdles of Web 3.0, it's crucial to address the challenge of regulation. Without a defined legal framework and policy guidance, Web 3.0's global expansion will inevitably face limitations.

Like any new technology that radically shifts existing industries, growing pains are inevitable. Not all challenges can be solved technologically. Without a clear legal framework and policy guidance, traditional institutions and organizations lack a definitive path to follow and are hesitant to engage with and invest in the Web 3.0 ecosystem. Establishing legal frameworks and policy guidance that protect innovation through industry collaboration could encourage institutions and organizations to commit to Web 3.0, serving as service providers or integrating their existing customer bases.

In the United States, the government has adopted proactive, innovation-supportive regulatory policies to stay ahead, using executive orders and local legislation to foster Web 3.0 development, creating frameworks for qualitative and innovative regulation.

China supports blockchain innovation and application but bans decentralized financial activities, promoting blockchain and digital RMB while strictly restricting trading and ICOs and treating them as illegal financial activities. In China, consortium chains are taxable, but mining is banned.

The EU's crypto-friendly regulatory stance supports innovation and eco-friendliness, recognizing tokens as legal property and allowing cryptocurrencies to exist in various forms, with temporary tax exemptions on cryptocurrency-related activities.

South Korea's government supports legal digital assets, banning ICOs while requiring exchanges to obtain government approval and planning to tax digital asset capital gains from 2023.

Singapore, a regulatory pioneer, adopts a supportive stance, categorizing tokens and offering compliance licenses, exempting cryptocurrency-related goods and services tax.

Current regulations focus mainly on blockchain and related financial activities. However, future Web 3.0 regulations need to cover digital identity sovereignty, personal data rights, and data transaction regulation.

In today's Web 2.0 era, centralized storage of digital identity information poses misuse and infringement risks. Web 3.0 promises more individual control and privacy, necessitating robust security and privacy mechanisms to prevent identity theft or misuse. Personal data, becoming a vital asset in Web 3.0, will require comprehensive protection frameworks to prevent unauthorized access or use, safeguarding data sovereignty and privacy.

Regulating data transactions is also crucial for Web 3.0, addressing potential misuse, infringement, and improper transactions. Regulators must establish clear legal frameworks for data trading, ensuring fairness, justice, and safety in data exchange and promoting rational data utilization.

While government regulation can enhance Web 3.0 transparency, accountability, consumer protection, and innovation, attracting compliant investment institutions, it can also slow innovation and limit freedom of speech. Balancing innovation and regulation is key to maximizing benefits and minimizing drawbacks in Web 3.0's evolution.

7.3 The Inevitable Arrival of the Web 3.0 Era

The arrival of the Web 3.0 era is inevitable and irreversible. To many today, Web 3.0 may seem abstract and distant, with some of its underlying technologies still far from commercialization or mature application.

However, whether viewed from the perspective of technological trends or the direction of human civilization's evolution, we are destined to move toward the Web 3.0 era.

Technologically, with the rapid advancement of various digital technologies like the IoT, AI, and the metaverse, society is gradually transitioning into an era of digital twins. In this era, we are not merely biological beings but also possess digital counterparts. The advent of the digital twin era will inevitably lead to the rise of digital identity and sovereignty, awakening an era of digital sovereignty consciousness where the importance of individual data ownership and control is recognized.

As this awareness strengthens, it will catalyze resistance against the data monopolies of centralized platforms. People will start to question whether centralized data management aligns with individual interests and societal fairness and development. This will drive the search for new business models based on digital identity sovereignty and personal data rights, reshaping the flow and utilization of data—what we refer to as Web 3.0 today.

From a civilizational perspective, achieving Web 3.0 means actualizing digital sovereignty and viewing users as individuals rather than cogs in the data economy. Although Web 2.0 remains powerful, with websites boasting billions of users and market values in the tens of billions, the underlying logic of its strength—excessive centralization of user data and assets—is failing. Web 2.0 giants often pride themselves on having vast user accounts and data but overlook the user rights infringed by such centralized control.

In the past, people sought Internet convenience, neglecting issues like digital identity, privacy rights, and data assets, leading to a few giants monopolizing the Internet. For example, the Internet's development has made sharing so commonplace that many no longer discern between public and private realms. Many parents, for instance, share photos of their children online without considering whether their children would appreciate those images being permanent and publicly accessible.

Many data breaches and privacy exposures are partly due to platforms, but often, we also relinquish our privacy protection. Unaware of the risks, many navigate the Internet believing in its safety, oblivious to the potential for their online traces to be accessed. Fortunately, more businesses and individuals are becoming aware of these issues and valuing data ownership and rights. Corporate awakening is just the beginning; small and large businesses, individuals, and all society members will demand autonomous identities, data, social relationships, assets, and rights. This trend is irreversible.

While resistance against centralized giants is still feeble, particularly in highly concentrated fields like social networking and short videos, discontent and anger are accumulating. Every abuse of power by platforms accelerates the end of Web 2.0 and lays the groundwork for Web 3.0's rise.

People's changing mindsets and ideologies, once initiated, are irreversible. Though this shift is still subtle and slow—owing to the immature state of Web 3.0 technology, even the definition of Web 3.0 is becoming vague and broad—the concept has evolved significantly. Initially, discussions around Web 3.0 centered on blockchain technology. However, from a cutting-edge tech perspective, it's clear that blockchain, despite playing a significant role, isn't the sole driver of Web 3.0. Blockchain's decentralization, immutability, and security are valuable, but its limitations—insufficient performance, high energy consumption, and poor scalability—highlight the need for broader and diverse technological support, including AI, quantum computing, IoT, and quantum communication. These technologies' integration will actualize the open, transparent, secure, and privacy-focused digital world envisioned by Web 3.0.

Now, as Web 3.0's concepts are being refined, with a focus on solving real-world issues, the technology and infrastructure are poised for rapid development, promising a transformative industry landscape. Once people taste the benefits of autonomous identity, data, and assets, there will be no turning back to the Web 2.0 world.

After all, owning an autonomous identity enables individuals to manage their information freely, ensuring greater privacy and security. Autonomous data ownership allows for more flexible data management and utilization, safeguarding privacy and rights. And possessing autonomous assets grants individuals freedom in managing and utilizing their digital wealth, free from traditional financial monopolies.

Once the advantages of autonomous identity, data, and assets are experienced, not only will people be unwilling to return to the Web 2.0 realm, but they'll also actively support and contribute to building and developing the Web 3.0 ecosystem, striving for digital freedom and innovation. With policy and regulatory involvement, once regulators start employing Web 3.0's mechanisms, Web 2.0's regulatory methods will become outdated, as Web 3.0's frameworks are better suited for the digital and decentralized landscape, ensuring market participant protection and stability.

In essence, as mindsets and ideologies shift, the transformation becomes unstoppable. From corporations to individuals and from small businesses to consumers, everyone is seeking liberation from centralized control. This transformative wave is irreversible. The philosophy of Web 3.0 is rapidly spreading, and people will eventually realize that true digital freedom and innovation can only be achieved on the foundation of digital identity sovereignty and personal data rights.

Regardless of our belief, acceptance, or willingness, the Internet is bound to enter a new era driven by a confluence of cutting-edge technologies. This transition is a technological inevitability, a historical certainty, and a commercial inevitability. From Web 1.0 to 2.0 and now toward 3.0, the future may hold 4.0, 5.0, or beyond. Currently, Web 3.0 is the foreseeable future we can envision. What comes after Web 3.0, whether we continue with Web technologies or evolve into something entirely new under the influence of disruptive technologies, is a story that only the future can reveal.

References

a15a. *Understanding Web 3.0: Blockchain, NFT, Metaverse, and DAO*. Edited by OxAres.

Ali, Anwar Adeem. "A Survey of Semantic Web (Web 3.0), Its Applications, Challenges, Future, and Its Relation with Internet of Things (IoT)." *Web Intelligence* (2022).

Bharadiya, Jasmin Praful. "Artificial Intelligence and the Future of Web 3.0: Opportunities and Challenges Ahead." *American Journal of Computer Science and Technology*, no. 2 (2023).

Cai, Wanhuan, and Zhang Zizhu. "Data as a Production Factor: Data Capitalization, Profit Distribution, and Ownership." *Teaching and Research*, no. 07 (2022): 57–65.

Chen, Long. "Labor Order under 'Digital Control': A Study on the Labor Control of Food Delivery Riders." *Sociological Studies* 35, no. 06 (2020): 113–135, 244. doi:10.19934/j.cnki.shxyj.2020.06.006.

Cheng, Shenghui, Huang Tianyi, Meng Yiran, et al. "The Development Opportunities and Challenges of Web 3.0." *Science & Technology Review* 41, no. 15 (2023): 22–35.

Cheng, Shenghui. *Web 3.0: The Third-Generation Internet with Disruptive and Significant Opportunities.*

References

Fred. "Exploring the Paths of Web3 Social: A Flash in the Pan or the Next Mass Adoption?"

Han, Xuan, Yuan Yong, and Wang Feiyue. "Security Issues in Blockchain: Current Status and Future Prospects." *Acta Automatica Sinica* 45, no. 01 (2019): 206–225. doi:10.16383/j.aas.c180710.

Huang, Yifan. "Exploring the Evolutionary Characteristics of Internet Media from Web 1.0 to Web 3.0." *Digital Communication World*, no. 02 (2023): 33–35.

Jiang, Dong, Yuan Ye, Zhang Xiaowei, et al. "A Survey of Data Pricing and Trading Research." *Journal of Software* 34, no. 03 (2023): 1396–1424. doi:10.13328/j.cnki.jos.006751.

Li, J., and Wang F. "The TAO of Blockchain Intelligence for Intelligent Web 3.0." *IEEE/CAA Journal of Automatica Sinica* 10, no. 12 (2023): 2183–2186.

Li, Juanjuan, Qin Rui, Ding Wenwen, et al. "A New Framework for Decentralized Autonomous Organizations and Operations Based on Web3." *Acta Automatica Sinica* 49, no. 05 (2023): 985–998. doi:10.16383/j.aas.c220753.

Li, Zeyuan. "A New Outlook on the Digital Economy from the Perspective of Marx's Labor Theory of Value: Taking Web 3.0 and Digital Labor as Examples." *Business Economics*, no. 16 (2023): 79–82. doi:10.19995/j.cnki.CN10-1617/F7.2023.16.079.

Ling, Jingqi. "In the Era of WEB 3.0, Should Fashion Be Reset?—the Production and Marketing Model and Value System of NFT Digital Fashion Goods." *Fashion Designer*, no. 06 (2022): 10–16.

Major Data Strategy Key Laboratory. *Redefining Big Data*.

Mario, Gabriele. "DAO Penetration of the Internet: The New Organizational Paradigm of Web 3.0."

Meyer-Schönberger, Viktor. *The Age of Big Data*.

Newman, Russell, Victor Chang, Robert John Walters, and Gary Brian Wills. "Web 2.0—the Past and the Future." *International Journal of Information Management* (2016).

Peng, Lan. "The Evolution of 'Connectivity': The Basic Logic of Internet Evolution." *International Journalism* 35, no. 12 (2013): 6–19. doi:10.13495/j.cnki.cjjc.2013.12.001.

References

Peng, Xiaozhun, and Dong Chenchen. "Web 3.0, Metaverse, and the Development of Financial Technology." *Era of Financial Technology* 30, no. 08 (2022): 18–26.

Qu, Jiabao. "New Changes and Contradictions in the Reproduction of Labor Force under the Perspective of Digital Capitalism." *Contemporary Economic Research*, no. 12 (2020): 13–23.

Rudman, Riaan, and Bruwer Rikus. "Defining Web 3.0: Opportunities and Challenges." *The Electronic Library* (2016).

Sadowski, Jathan. "The Internet of Landlords: Digital Platforms and New Mechanisms of Rentier Capitalism." *Antipode* (2020).

Srnicek, Nick. *Platform Capitalism.*

SupraOracles. "A Detailed Explanation: The Differences Between Web 1.0, Web 2.0, and Web 3.0."

Wang, Hanyang. "Can the Internet Still Improve? Geek Spirit and Web 3."

Wang, Yanan, and Zhang Yinghua. "From Platform Economy to Creator Economy: Research on the Reconstruction Path of Digital Content Production System in the Era of Web 3.0." *Publishing Research*, no. 04 (2023): 31–36. doi:10.19393/j.cnki.cn11-1537/g2.2023.04.035.

Yao, Qian. "Web 3.0: The Gradually Approaching New Generation of the Internet." *China Finance*, no. 06 (2022): 14–17.

Yu, Bin. "An Analysis of the Political Economy of 'Digital Labor' and 'Digital Capital.'" *Marxist Studies*, no. 05 (2021): 77–86, 152.

Zhou, Yanyun, and Yan Xiurong. *Digital Labor and Karl Marx.* Beijing: China Social Sciences Press, 2016.

Index

KEVIN CHEN is a renowned science and technology writer and scholar. He was a visiting scholar at Columbia University, a postdoctoral scholar at the University of Cambridge, and an invited course professor at Peking University. He has served as a special commentator and columnist for the *People's Daily*, CCTV, China Business Network, SINA, NetEase, and many other media outlets. He has published monographs in numerous domains, including finance, science and technology, real estate, medical treatments, and industrial design. He currently lives in Hong Kong.